MATH TRAILBLAZERS™

A Mathematical Journey Using Science and Language Arts

Student Guide

Grade 2

A TIMS® Curriculum from
University of Illinois at Ch...

KENDALL/HUNT PUBLISHING COMPANY
4050 Westmark Drive   Dubuque, Iowa 52002

MATH TRAILBLAZERS™

Dedication

This book is dedicated to the children and
teachers who let us see the magic
in their classrooms
and to our families who wholeheartedly
supported us while we searched for
ways to make it happen.

The TIMS Project

UIC The University of Illinois
at Chicago

This material is based on work supported by the National Science Foundation under grant
No. MDR 9050226 and the University of Illinois at Chicago. Any opinions, findings, and
conclusions or recommendations expressed in this publication are those of the author(s)
and do not necessarily reflect the views of the granting agencies.

Printed in the United States of America
10 9 8 7 6

Acknowledgments

TIMS Elementary Mathematics Curriculum Project

Director and Co-Principal Investigator
Philip Wagreich

Co-Principal Investigator
Howard Goldberg

Associate Director
Joan L. Bieler

TIMS Senior Curriculum Developers

Janet Simpson Beissinger
Howard Goldberg
Catherine Randall Kelso

Astrida Cirulis
Carol Inzerillo
Leona Peters

Marty Gartzman
Andy Isaacs
Philip Wagreich

TIMS Curriculum Developers

Janice C. Banasiak
Kathryn Chval
Sandy Niemiera

Lynne Beauprez
Diane R. Czerwinski
Polly Tangora

Lindy M. Chambers
Janice Ozima
Paul Trafton

Research Consultant
Andy Isaacs

Mathematics Education Consultant
Paul Trafton

Editors
Jay Becker
Lynelle Morgenthaler

Designer/Production Coordinator
Sarah Nelson

Production Staff

Glenda Genio   Mini Joseph   Sarah Nelson   Biruté Petrauskas

Illustrator
Kris Dresen

National Advisory Committee

- Carl Berger, Director, Instructional Technology, University of Michigan, Ann Arbor, Michigan
- Tom Berger, Professor of Mathematics Education, Colby College, Waterville, Maine
- Hugh Burkhardt, Project Director, Balanced Assessment for the Mathematics Curriculum, University of California, Berkeley and Shell Centre for Mathematical Education, University of Nottingham, England
- Donald Chambers, Director of Dissemination, National Center for Research in Mathematical Sciences Education, University of Wisconsin at Madison, Madison, Wisconsin
- Naomi Fisher, Co-Director, Mathematicians and Education Reform Network, University of Illinois at Chicago, Chicago, Illinois
- Glenda Lappan, Professor of Mathematics, Michigan State University, East Lansing, Michigan
- Mary Lindquist, Callaway Professor of Mathematics Education, Columbus College, Columbus, Georgia
- Eugene Maier, President, Math Learning Center, Portland, Oregon
- Lourdes Monteagudo, Director, Teachers' Academy for Mathematics and Science, Chicago, Illinois
- Elizabeth Phillips, Specialist in the Department of Mathematics, Michigan State University, East Lansing, Michigan
- Thomas Post, Professor of Mathematics Education, University of Minnesota, Minneapolis, Minnesota

Acknowledgments

Research and Outreach Staff

Birch Burghardt
Marty Gartzman

Andy Carter
Michelle Perry

Barbara Crum
Maria Varelas

Teacher Contributors

Jean Clement
Donna Holt

Ann Watson Cohn
Jenny Knight
Beth Savage

Catherine Hamilton
Mary Pat Larocca

Institute for Mathematics and Science Education Support Staff

David Browdy
Shanila Dada
Helen Gary
Judy Kim
Alex Mak
Enrique Puente
Leah Rosenstein
Patty Stevenson
Marie Walz

Jocelyn Buchanan
Robert Denton
Byron S. Gudiel
Frannie Los Banes
Christie Manisto
Laura Ratcliffe
Ellen Rydell
Ami Thaker
Mikka Whiteaker

Philomina Cox
Nadine Dombrowski
Miriam Gutierrez
Cassandra Lucas
Kim Meyer
Monica Rodriguez
Dorothy Sholeen-Modrzyk
Greg Waddoups

Copyeditor
Anne Roby

Video and Photographic Documentation

Joan L. Bieler

Henrique Cirne-Lima

Paul A. Wussow

Contributing Writers and Artists

Steven Bloom
Karen Harrington
Heather Miller

Pam Conrad
Vida Ivancevic
Betty Romanek

Julie Hall
Songgu Kwon
Cora Lee Wentzel

Field Test Schools and Teachers

Abraham Lincoln School, Oak Park, Illinois
Principal: Carol Dudzik

Sandra Adams
Peggy Callahan
Catherine Hamilton
Donna Holt
Susan McNish
Karl Radnitzer
Shirley Warner

Marilyn Blenz
Susan Casagrande
James Harrington
Paula Hughes
Miraflor Metropoulos
Jane Samuelson
Kathleen Wiedow

Nell Bloyd
Cheryl Cohen
Karen Heffner
Frank LoCoco
Joyce Moore
Jarvia Thomas
Lynne Zillman

Anderson Elementary School, Chicago, Illinois
Principal: Marie Iska
Alicia Acevedo

Acknowledgments

Daniel Boone School, Chicago, Illinois
Principal: Paul Zavitkovsky

Sybil Bennin
Deanna Gramatis
Paula Hyman
Mila Kell
Janice Ozima
Dixie Rouleau
Jennifer Soro
Lauretta Williams

Ruta Buntinas
Susan Dietz
Sandra Kantz
Julia Kline
Vlada Polin
Mariah Seton
Cheryl Strong
Constance Winschel-Cook
Argentina Yousif

Myung Chi
Norma Duarte
Juliet Kasha
Barbara Mandel
Lizette Rhone
Cecilia Somma
Margaret Therriault-Jenkins
Elina Yelishevich

Drexel School, Cicero, Illinois
Principal: Cliff Pluister

Deborah Fantozzi

Jeanette Ibarra

Kristin Wilderman

Edith Wolford Elementary School, Colorado Springs, Colorado
Principal: Gary Langenhuizen

Sherrie Antes
Carol Eames

Karen Combs
Kelly Garnhart

Jeremy Cramer

Edward H. White School, Chicago, Illinois
Principal: Yvonne Womack

Judy Hobson

Harrison Jackson

Kathleen Pidrak

Elmwood School, Elmwood Park, Illinois
Principal: Doug Lia

Joanne Hoffmann

Mary Anne Kirsch

Linda Norris

Marlene Ryan

Emma Stark Hampton Elementary School, Detroit, Michigan
Principal: Chrystal Tibbs

Margaret Erle
Clare Whitaker

Janet Flessa
Michelle Williams

Therese Sadlier

Gavin Central School, Ingleside, Illinois
Principal: Theresa Dunkin

Nannette Borzewski
Carrie Frebault
Peggy Owczarski

Judith Dahl
Jennifer McCracken
Pat Scully
Dawn Smith

Betty Denk
Jodi Minsky
Barbara Smejkal

Hammerschmidt Elementary School, Lombard, Illinois
Principal: James Adams

Shelly Humphreys

James McCosh School, Chicago, Illinois
Principal: Barbara Eason-Watkins

Louise Dearman
Inez Jacobson

Leah Fulton
Dorothy Turner

Shelley Hefner
Jacquelyne White

Acknowledgments

James Shields School, Chicago, Illinois
Principal: Rita Gardner

Julie Cartwright
Wilhelmina McGee

Iris Delgado
Terry McInerney

Bob Kaszynski
Maranielly Vazquez

John C. Burroughs School, Chicago, Illinois
Principal: Richard Morris
Paul Durkin
Michelle Sanborn

John Mills School, Elmwood Park, Illinois
Principal: Patricia Duggan

Deanna Crum   Lisa Loffredo   Cathy McGovern   Bonnie Mize

Mt. Hope Elementary School, Lansing, Michigan
Principal: Betty Nichols

Corin Bennett
Della Gregory
Sue Usiak

Deidre Bennett
Geneva Martin
Terri Weinlander

Sue Fillingham
Deborah Muth
Dawn Vanzee

Piedmont Elementary School, Charleston, West Virginia
Principal: Steve Knighton

Beth Brown
Eva Jones

Brigid Haney
Louise Tabor

Catherine Hastings

Pilsen Community Academy, Chicago, Illinois
Principal: Ana Espinoza

Jennifer Chadwick   Judy Rappin   Juliet Rempa

Spring Hill School, Roselle, Illinois
Principal: Sally Pryor
David R. Vilmin

St. Ambrose School, Chicago, Illinois
Principal: Sr. Dolores Lytle
Dorothy Rivers

Westwood Primary School, Phoenix, Arizona
Principal: Martha Braly

Denise Ahart
Merrillyn Curtis
Alphine Glenn
Nancy Hunt
Candace Manger
Lori Perry
Anita Rothman
Kathy Schaeffer
Susie Sweeney

Denise Arnold
Antoinette DiCarlo
Nancy Herbert
Cecilia Kelly
Diane Nonack
Denise Pizzi
JoAnn Salem
Ken Schofield
Jamie Tinkelman
Nan Williams

Shelley Carson
Ginny Fields
Jane Hoyle
Cindy Lauersdorf
Kathie Pabst
Maureen Riordan
Timothy Salem
Sheri Starke
Jackie Williams

William H. Ray School, Chicago, Illinois
Principal: Cydney Fields
Bill Salvato
Marie Schilling

Table of Contents

Additional student pages may be found in the *Discovery Assignment Book,*
Adventure Book, or the *Unit Resource Guide.*

Table of Contents

Additional student pages may be found in the *Discovery Assignment Book,*
Adventure Book, or the *Unit Resource Guide.*

Dear Parents,

MATH TRAILBLAZERS™ is based on the belief that all children deserve a challenging mathematics curriculum and that mathematics is best learned through solving many different kinds of problems. The program provides a careful balance of concepts and skills. Traditional arithmetic skills and procedures are covered through their repeated use in problems and through distributed practice.

MATH TRAILBLAZERS™, however, offers much more. Students using this program will become proficient problem solvers, will know how to approach problems in many different ways, will know when and how to apply the mathematics they have learned, and will be able to clearly communicate their mathematical knowledge. They will learn more mathematics than in a traditional program—computation, measurement, geometry, data collection and analysis, estimation, graphing, patterns and relationships, mental arithmetic, and simple algebraic ideas are all an integral part of the curriculum. They will see connections between the mathematics learned in school and the mathematics used in everyday life. And, they will enjoy and value the work they do in mathematics.

This curriculum was built around national recommendations for improving mathematics instruction in American schools and the research that supported those recommendations. It has been extensively tested with thousands of children in dozens of classrooms over five years of development. **MATH TRAILBLAZERS™** reflects our view of a complete and well-balanced mathematics program that will prepare children for a world in the 21st century where proficiency in mathematics will be a necessity. We hope that you enjoy this exciting approach to learning mathematics as you watch your child's mathematical abilities grow throughout the year.

Philip Wagreich

Philip Wagreich
Teaching Integrated Mathematics and Science Project
University of Illinois at Chicago
Chicago, Illinois

UNIT 1

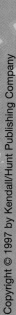
1

Ms. Carter's Class

Ms. Carter's class used the information in the data table to make a graph. Use the graph to answer questions on the following page.

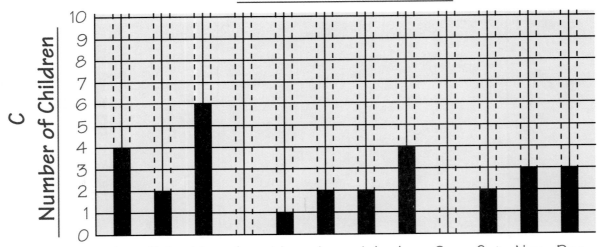

Birth Months

Birth Month

B

Birth Months

Ms. Carter's Class

1. What is the most common birth month in Ms. Carter's class? How do you know?

_____

_____

2. What is the least common birth month(s)? _____

3. How many children have birthdays in August? _____

4. Which months have the same number of birthdays?

_____

5. How many students are in Ms. Carter's class? _____

6. Is Ms. Carter's class larger, smaller, or the same size as your class? How do you know?

_____

_____

7. How does your class graph differ from Ms. Carter's class graph?

_____

_____

_____

Animal Problems

1. Five kittens are playing with a ball of string. Three kittens are eating.

   How many kittens are in the litter? _____

2. A pod of whales has 3 males and 9 females.

   How many whales are in the pod? _____

3. A pig has 9 piglets in her litter. She already fed five of the piglets, and the rest are hungry.

   How many hungry piglets are there? _____

4. A pack of wolves has 5 adults and 8 pups.

   How many wolves live in this pack? _____

5. There was a herd of elephants. Three baby elephants were born. Now there are seven elephants.

   How many elephants were in the herd to start? _____

6. There were 11 chattering monkeys. Four fell asleep.

   How many monkeys are still chattering? _____

7. There were 12 toads sitting near the pond. Some jumped away. Four toads are still sitting near the pond.

   How many toads jumped away? _____

Animal Trading Cards

Pod of Whales	Troop of Monkeys	Pride of Lions	Parliament of Owls
4¢	5¢	6¢	7¢

Solve the problems. Write a number sentence for each.

1. Michelle bought a Pod of Whales card and a Pride of Lions card. How much did she spend?

_____

2. Loni bought two Pride of Lions cards. How much did she spend?

_____

3. Katrina spent 11¢. What did she buy?

_____

4. Freddie spent 9¢. What did he buy?

_____

5. Tony bought three cards and spent 15¢. What did he buy?

_____

Name _____ Date _____

More Animal Trading Cards

Work with your partner to discuss and solve the problems.
Write a number sentence for each.

Pod of Whales	Troop of Monkeys	Pride of Lions	Parliament of Owls
4¢	5¢	6¢	7¢

1. Lowell bought three cards. Two of the cards are the same. He spent 16¢. What did he buy? Find two solutions.

_____

2. Bill bought 3 different cards. He spent more than 15¢. What did he buy? Find two solutions.

_____

3. Martina had 17¢. She bought three cards and had 3¢ left. What did she buy? Find two solutions.

_____

4. Sara bought three cards and spent 18¢. What did she buy? Find three solutions.

_____

Six Solutions

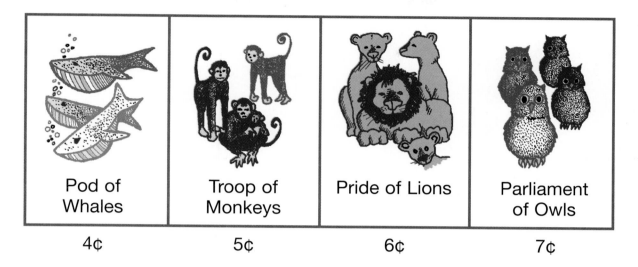

Pod of Whales	Troop of Monkeys	Pride of Lions	Parliament of Owls
4¢	5¢	6¢	7¢

Shanta bought three cards and spent more than 17¢. Find six different solutions. Write a number sentence for each. You can buy more than one of each card.

1. _____

2. _____

3. _____

4. _____

5. _____

6. _____

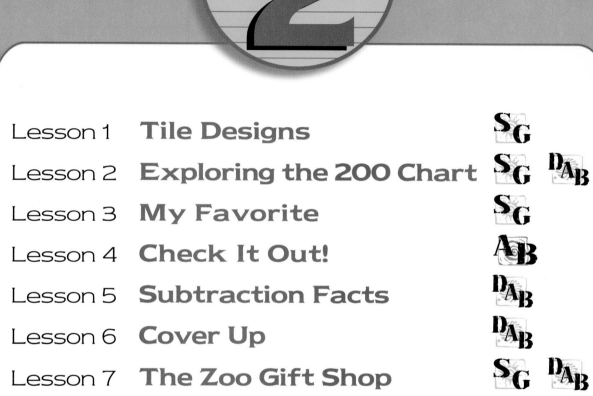

UNIT 2

What's My Number Sentence?

Write two number sentences for each tile design.

1A. _____

1B. _____

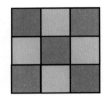

2A. _____

2B. _____

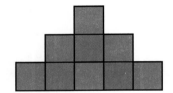

3A. _____

3B. _____

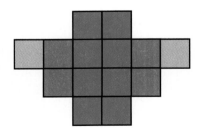

4A. _____

4B. _____

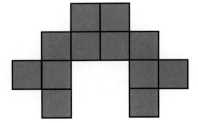

5A. _____

5B. _____

Make Your Own Tile Design

Make a design on the grid with tiles. Record your design by removing the tiles and coloring the squares.

Write your number sentences on a separate sheet of paper.

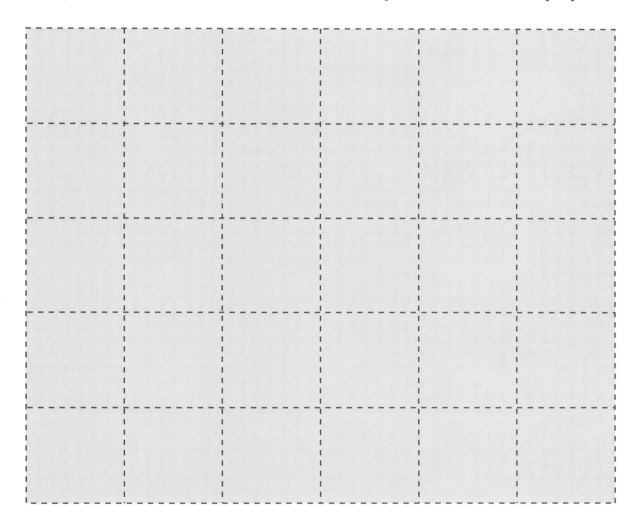

Miko's Tile Design

Miko made this design using color tiles. She
wrote this number sentence to describe it.
1 + 2 + 3 + 2 + 1 = 9

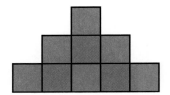

Her friend Amy wrote another number
sentence for the design. 1 + 3 + 5 = 9

1. Tell how Miko and Amy were looking at the design when
   they wrote these number sentences.

   Miko

   _____

   _____

   Amy

   _____

   _____

2. Write a different number sentence to describe Miko's
   design.

   _____

200 Chart

1	2	3	4	5	6	7	8	9	10
11	12	13	14	15	16	17	18	19	20
21	22	23	24	25	26	27	28	29	30
31	32	33	34	35	36	37	38	39	40
41	42	43	44	45	46	47	48	49	50
51	52	53	54	55	56	57	58	59	60
61	62	63	64	65	66	67	68	69	70
71	72	73	74	75	76	77	78	79	80
81	82	83	84	85	86	87	88	89	90
91	92	93	94	95	96	97	98	99	100
101	102	103	104	105	106	107	108	109	110
111	112	113	114	115	116	117	118	119	120
121	122	123	124	125	126	127	128	129	130
131	132	133	134	135	136	137	138	139	140
141	142	143	144	145	146	147	148	149	150
151	152	153	154	155	156	157	158	159	160
161	162	163	164	165	166	167	168	169	170
171	172	173	174	175	176	177	178	179	180
181	182	183	184	185	186	187	188	189	190
191	192	193	194	195	196	197	198	199	200

Moving on the 200 Chart

To play this game, you and your partner need:

- A spinner;
- A scorecard;
- A 200 chart.

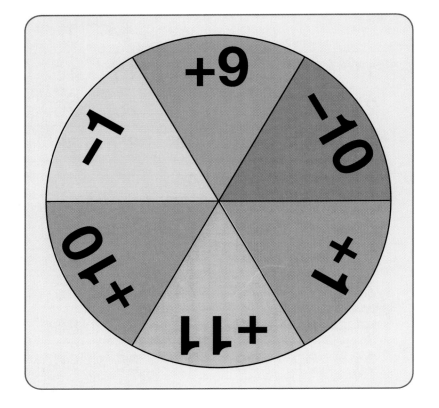

Directions

Begin at 50 on the 200 chart. Spin, and do what the spin tells you. Record your spin and your new number on your scorecard. Take turns with your partner until your scorecard is full. The partner with the biggest number at the end wins!

Moving on the 200 Chart Scorecard

Player 1 _____
Start with 50.

Player 2 _____
Start with 50.

Spin	New Number

Spin	New Number

Name ______________________ Date ______________

Missing 200 Chart Numbers

Homework

Dear Family Member:

Your child has been working on patterns and relationships in the number system using a 200 chart. Refer to the 200 Chart in the Student Guide. Each square below represents a section of the chart with numbers missing. As shown in the example, a move up decreases the number by ten, down increases it by ten, left decreases it by one, and right increases it by one.

Thank you for your cooperation.

Write the missing numbers in the pieces of the 200 chart below.

1	2	3
11	12	13
21	22	23

Example

	27	
		38

	73	
	83	

78		
	89	

Mr. Hart's Class

Mr. Hart's class used the information in the data table to make a graph.

Our Favorite Taco

T Type of Taco	C Number of Children
Steak	6
Chicken	7
Beef	9
Pork	0
Veggie	2
Avocado	3

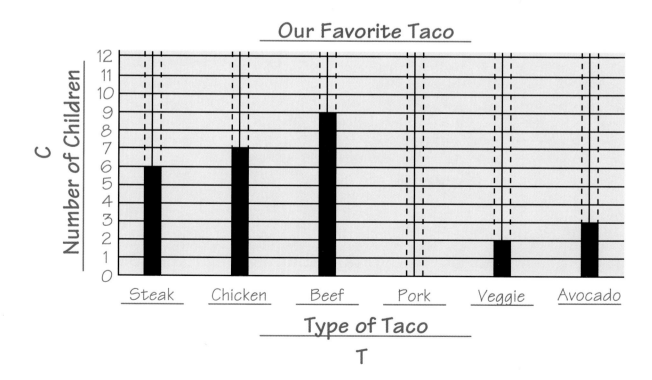

Our Favorite Taco

Mr. Hart's Class

1. What is the most popular type of taco in Mr. Hart's class? How do you know?

   _____

   _____

2. What type of taco is the least favorite?

   _____

3. How many children chose chicken tacos as their favorite?

   _____

4. How many students are in Mr. Hart's class?

   _____

5. Mr. Hart ordered one taco for each of his students. The cashier put the veggie and the avocado tacos in one bag. All of the steak tacos were placed in a second bag. Which bag has more tacos? How many more?

   _____

6. The day after Mr. Hart's class graphed this data, two new students were added to the class. Joe and Anita both chose pork tacos as their favorite. Change the data table and graph to show Joe and Anita's data.

Zoo Gift Shop Animal Figures

Fill in prices for the animals below.

UNIT 3

How Would You Sort Them?

Sort the following buttons. Describe how you would sort them below.

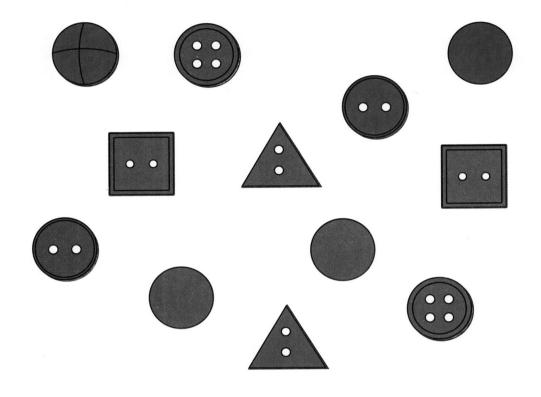

_____

_____

_____

_____

_____

_____

All Sorts of Buttons

Button Sizer

Use the boxes to decide if your buttons are small, medium, or large.

If a button fits in this box, it is <u>small</u>.

If a button fits in this box, it is <u>medium</u>.

If a button fits in this box, it is <u>large</u>.

Size	Number of Buttons	Total
Small		
Medium		
Large		

Button Sizer Graph

Graph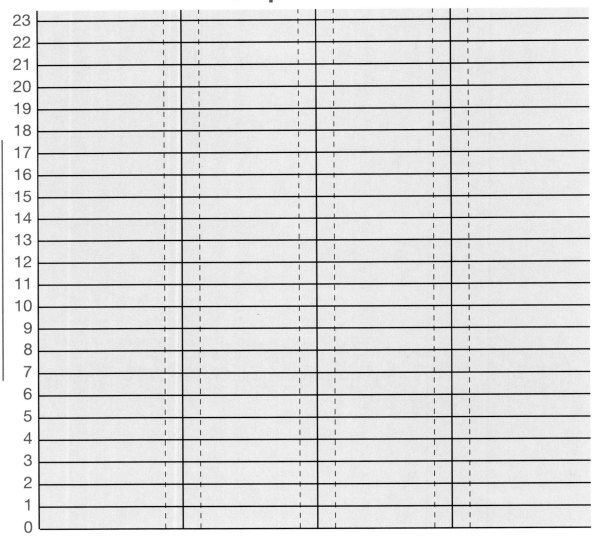

Use the information from your data table to complete the following graph.

Graph of Buttons

Size

Name _____   Date _____

Button Solutions

Solve each problem. Show how you found the answer.

1. Julia grabbed a handful of buttons. She had 8 red buttons, 6 blue buttons, and 7 orange buttons. How many buttons were in her handful?

2. Sarah had 22 buttons in her button collection. She gave 8 to Jeanette and 10 to Eric. How many buttons did she have left in her collection?

3. Stephen had a handful of buttons. He sorted them into groups of 5. There were four groups of five and two buttons left over. How many buttons were in Stephen's handful?

Bertha's Button Boutique

At Bertha's Button Boutique, you can buy many different types of buttons. The following cards show you four different kinds.

Card A	Card B	Card C	Card D
	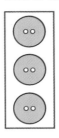	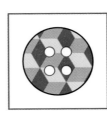	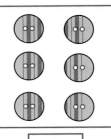
69¢	35¢	25¢	50¢

Solve each problem. Show how you found the answer.

1. Amanda bought Card A and Card B.
   How much did she spend?

   _____

2. Rachel bought two Card Bs.
   How many buttons did she get?

   _____

   How much did she spend?

   _____

3. Adan likes the buttons on Card D.
   If he buys two cards, how many buttons will he get?

   _____

4. Thomas bought a Card C and a Card D.
   How much did he spend?

   _____

Button Solutions

Button Place Value Tables

My group counted these buttons:

Hundreds	Tens	Ones

My group counted _____ buttons.

Our class counted these buttons:

Hundreds	Tens	Ones

Our class has a total of _____ buttons.

UNIT 4

High, Wide, and Handsome

Draw

Draw a picture of the lab. Be sure to show height *(H)* and arm span *(AS)*.

Collect

Measure the height and arm span for each student in your group.

Name	H Height (in _____) *unit*	AS Arm Span (in _____) *unit*

1. What is the shortest arm span in your group?

_____

2. What is the tallest height in your group?

_____

3. What is the difference between the tallest height and the shortest height?

_____

Arm Span Graph

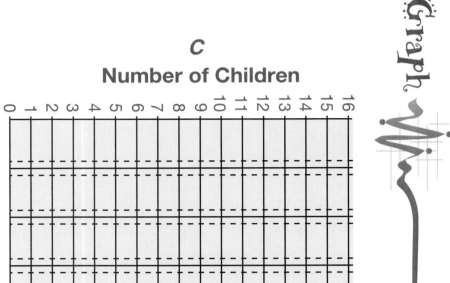

Graph

Number of Children
C

16
15
14
13
12
11
10
9
8
7
6
5
4
3
2
1
0

Arm Span (in links)
AS

Name _____ Date _____

Height Graph

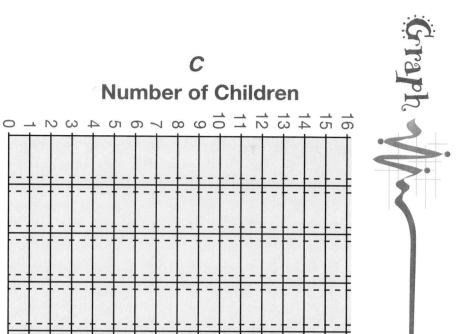

Graph

C
Number of Children

16
15
14
13
12
11
10
9
8
7
6
5
4
3
2
1
0

Height (in links)
H

Éxplore

Answer the following questions using the class data table.

1. Look at the tallest height and the shortest height. What is the range for height?

   _____

2. Look at the longest arm span and the shortest arm span. What is the range for arm span?

   _____

3. Maria's arm span is 33 links. How many links tall is Maria? Explain your thinking.

   _____

   _____

4. If you had identical twins in your class, would you expect their arm spans to be the same and their heights to be the same? Explain your thinking.

   _____

   _____

Three Rectangles

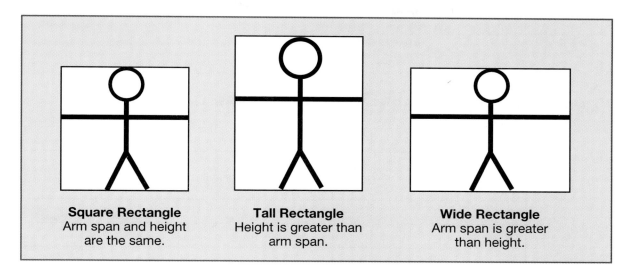

Square Rectangle
Arm span and height
are the same.

Tall Rectangle
Height is greater than
arm span.

Wide Rectangle
Arm span is greater
than height.

Complete the following sentences.

I am _____ links tall.

My arm span is _____ links.

The difference between my height and arm span is _____.

My height and arm span make a _____ rectangle shape.

Height and Arm Span Graph

Graph

Number the vertical axis. Then, graph the data.

L
Number of Links

Height
H

Arm
Span
AS

Type of Rectangle

Write the total of the tallies in the third column.

Miss Ozima's Class Rectangles

Type of Rectangle	Tallies	Total
Square Rectangle Arm span and height are the same.	ⅢⅠ Ⅲ̶Ⅰ Ⅲ	
Tall Rectangle Height is greater than arm span.	Ⅲ̶Ⅰ Ⅲ̶Ⅰ ⅢⅠ	
Wide Rectangle Arm span is greater than height.	ⅠⅠ	

Type of Rectangle

Graph

Use the information from Miss Ozima's class to make a bar graph. Number the vertical axis by ones.

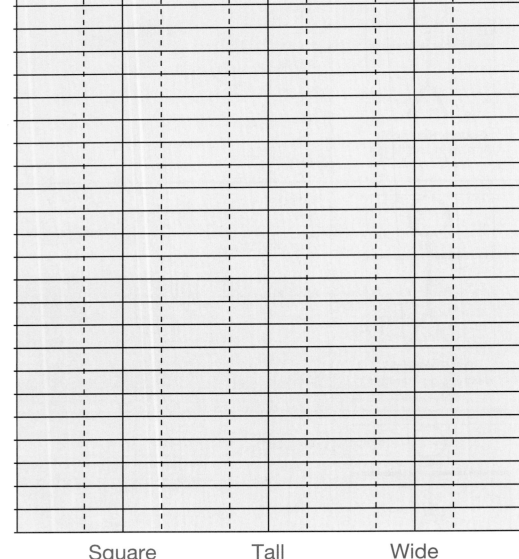

C
Number of Children

Square   Tall   Wide

Type of Rectangle
T

Hand Spans and Cubits

Measure each of the items listed below using your hand span. Then, measure them using your cubit. Measure two more objects or distances of your choice. Add them to the data table.

Object or Distance	Hand Spans	Cubits	
width of desk			
teacher's desk to door			
height of chalk rail			
teacher's desk to sharpener			
height of filing cabinet			

Choose a third measurement tool. Label the fourth column. Measure the objects and distances using this tool.

My Desk: Guess and Check

1. I estimate that the height of my desk is about

_____ hand spans.

2. Measure the height of your desk using hand spans. My desk is about

_____ hand spans.

3. Describe what you think about when you make an estimate.

_____

_____

_____

4. I estimate that the height of my desk is about _____ cubits.

5. Measure the height of your desk using cubits. My desk is

about _____ cubits.

6. Choose something else to measure in the room.

My _____ is about _____ hand spans.

My _____ is about _____ cubits.

When Close Is Good Enough

Could Be or Crazy?

Circle whether each statement "could be" true or if it is "crazy."

1. Tasha measured her dog's tail. It was 2 hand spans long.

   Could Be   Crazy

2. Fred is a second grader. He measured his height in cubits. He measured 30 cubits tall.

   Could Be   Crazy

3. Linda says her kitchen table is 4 cubits long. She says it is 4 hand spans long too.

   Could Be   Crazy

4. Connie said, "My hair is about 1 cubit long."

   Could Be   Crazy

5. Mark's dad says the width of the doorway is 5 hand spans. Mark, a second grader, measured 3 hand spans.

   Could Be   Crazy

6. Choose one of the statements. Explain how you decided if it was a "could be" or a "crazy" statement.

   _____

   _____

UNIT 5

Measurement Interval

Predict three lengths that fit in each interval. Then, use a chain of links to measure each length.

0–50 Links

Prediction	Length (in links)

51–100 Links

Prediction	Length (in links)

101–150 Links

Prediction	Length (in links)

The Long and Short of It

Name _____   Date _____

Where's My Location?

Fill in the missing numbers on each number line.

A.

0 1 2 3 4 __ 6 7 8 9 __ 11 12

B.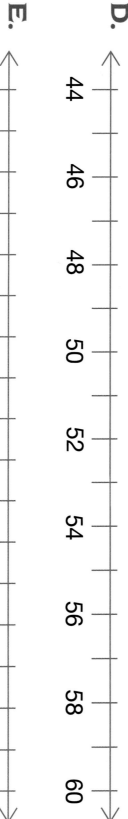

25 26 27 __ __ 30 31 __ __ __ __ 36 37 38

C.

90 91 92 __ __ __ __ __ 98 __ __ 101 __ 103

D.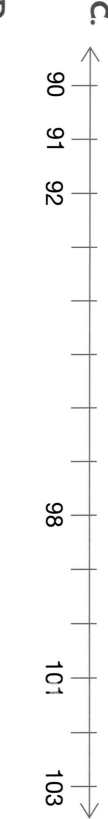

44 46 48 50 52 54 56 58 60

E.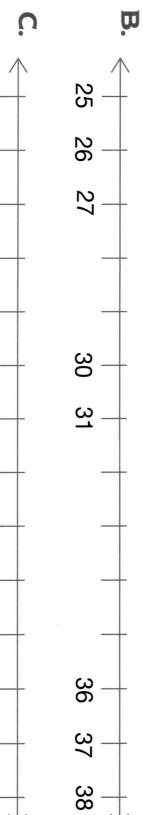

20 __ __ 25 __ __ __ 30 __ __ 35

Number Lines

As your teacher calls out numbers, write them on the number line.

Number Line for the Ages

H☺mＥwork

Dear Family Member:

The number line shows the numbers 1 to 100. Your child is learning to place numbers in the correct spot on the line. Help your child find the age of each family member and place the age in the correct place on the line. Your child will enjoy recording ages for several generations.

Thank you for your cooperation.

Record ages from your family on the number line.

```
0 ──┬── 10 ──┬── 20 ──┬── 30 ──┬── 40 ──┬── 50 ──┬── 60 ──┬── 70 ──┬── 80 ──┬── 90 ──┬── 100
```

My Own Number Line

```
├─┬─────┬─────┬─────┬─────┬─────┤
0    20    40    60    80    100
```

My number is _____. Place your number on the number line.

I know it goes where I put it because _____

_____

_____

_____

_____

_____

_____

_____

_____

Measuring Small

Use your meter tape or a meterstick.

1. How wide is your index finger? _____ cm

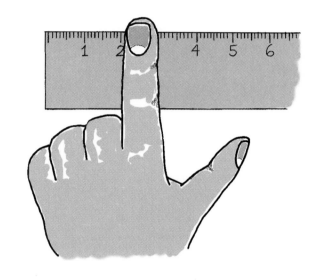

2. How long is the pencil? _____ cm

3. How long is this paper? _____ cm

4. Your choice: _____ _____ cm
   item name

Measuring Big

Use your paper meter tape or a meterstick.

1. How high is your desk?

   _____ cm

2. How tall are you? Have a classmate help measure your height.

   _____ cm

3. Are you exactly one meter tall?

   _____

4. Are you taller or shorter than one meter?

   _____

5. How high is it from the windowsill to the floor?

   _____ cm

   Is this exactly one meter? _____
   Is this more or less than one meter?

   _____

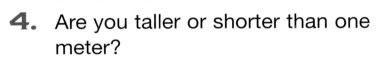

Centimeters and Meters

Estimating and Measuring

Find objects in the room. Estimate their lengths. Then, measure them.

Centimeters

Object	Estimation (centimeters)	Measurement (centimeters)
Eraser	5 cm	3 cm

Meters and Centimeters

Object	Estimation (m and cm)	Measurement (m and cm)

Tony at the Ballpark

Tony wrote the following story about measurements.

"My uncle took me to a baseball game. The White Sox played the Yankees. The ballpark was so big! We walked 80 **centimeters** to get to our seats. I bought a large soda about 1 **meter** tall and a hot dog 1 **hand span** long. The food was great! A White Sox player hit a home run. The ball must have gone 100 **centimeters**! A fan with a baseball glove 1 **meter** wide caught the ball. It was a wonderful day."

Complete the table using Tony's measurements. Which ones "could be" correct measurements, and which are "crazy"?

Object or Distance	Measurement	Could Be or Crazy
walk to seats		
large soda		
hot dog		
home run		
baseball glove		

Change Tony's story so it makes sense.

Rolling Along in Centimeters

Draw a picture to show how you will set up the lab. Be sure to show the two main variables.

What two main variables are we studying in this lab?

_____

What should stay the same each time the car is rolled?

_____

_____

Collect

Work with your group to test each car. Record your data in the table below.

T Type of Car	D Distance in _____ *unit*			
	Trial 1	Trial 2	Trial 3	Median
Sample				

Rolling Along in Centimeters

Graph

Make a bar graph of your data.

Explore

1. A. Which car rolled the longest distance?

_____

D = _____

B. Which car rolled the shortest distance?

_____

D = _____

C. What is the difference between the longest and the shortest distances? Show how you found your answer.

_____

2. You want to see which car is the best roller in the class. Can you tell using only your group's data table? Why or why not?

_____

_____

3. The teacher asked Debbie how far her car rolled. "It rolled 132," Debbie said. What is wrong with Debbie's answer?

_____

Rolling Along in Centimeters

Franco's Data

Franco's team found the data shown in the graph below.

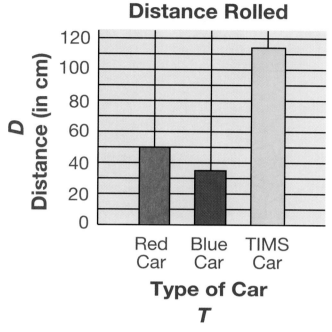

Distance Rolled

1. How far did the TIMS car roll?

_____

2. How much farther did the TIMS car roll than the Red Car?
Tell how you know.

_____

_____

3. Name at least one other thing you know by reading this
graph.

_____

_____

To the Hour

Write the times on the clocks below.

1.

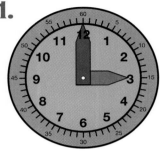

_____

2.

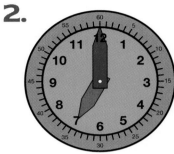

_____

3.

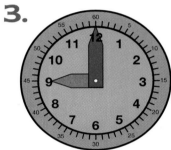

_____

4.

5.

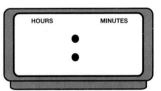

1:00

6.

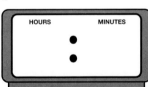

4:00

7.

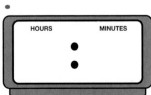

7 o'clock

8.

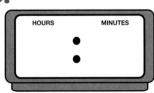

12 o'clock

Name _____ Date _____

To the Five Minute

Write the times on the clocks below.

1.

_____

2.

_____

3.

_____

4.
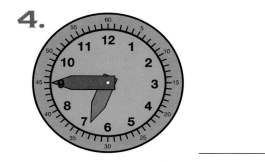
_____

5.
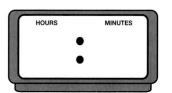
3:35

6.
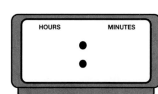
7:55

7.
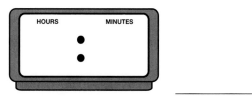
_____
"It's four fifteen."

8.
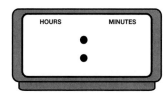
_____
"It's nine twenty."

Putting Them Together

Show the time on the analog or digital clock. Then, write the times shown. An example is done for you.

Example:

1.

2.

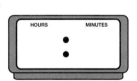

3.

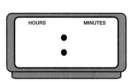

4.

Take Your Time

Take Your Time

Homework

Dear Family Member:

Your child is learning to tell time in school. Help your child tell the times on the clocks below. Thank you for your cooperation.

Write the time for the clocks below.

1.

_____

2.

_____

3.

_____

4.

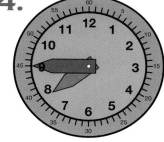

_____

5.

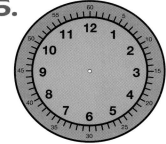

_____

"It's five fifty."

6.

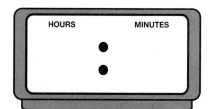

_____

"It's six twenty-five."

Time for Partners

Write the times shown on the clocks below.

1.

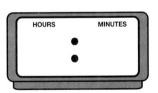

_____

2.

_____

3.

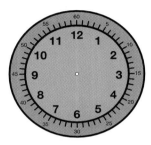

_____

4.

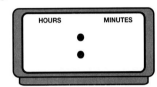

_____

Show the times on the clocks below.

5.

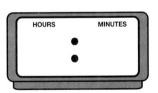

_____

6.

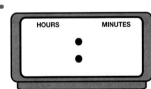

_____

7.

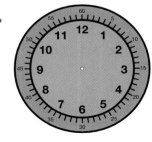

_____

8.

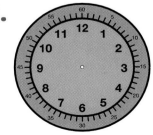

_____

Take Your Time

Marshmallows and Containers

Draw a picture of the experiment setup. Be sure to include the two main variables.

C Container	N Number of _____ *unit*

Graph

Make a graph of your data.

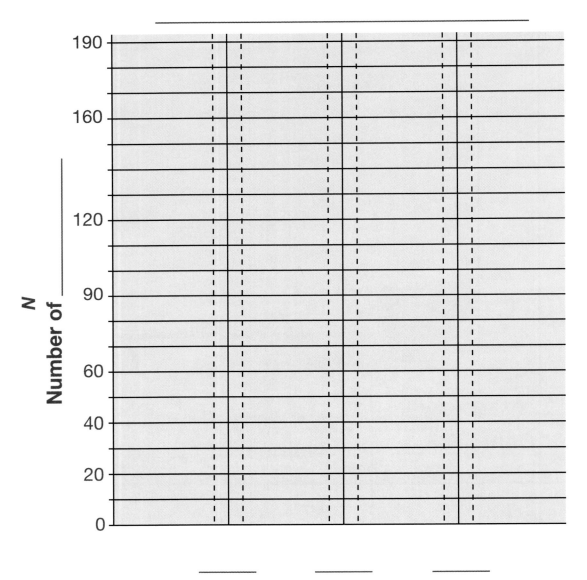

N
Number of _____

0 20 40 60 90 120 160 190

C
Container

Explore

Use the data table and graph to answer the questions below.

1. What are the two main variables in this experiment?

   _____

2. Which container is the tallest? _____

3. Which container is the widest? _____

4. Which container holds the most marshmallows? How do you know?

   _____

   _____

5. Which container has the largest volume? How do you know?

   _____

   _____

6. Which container has the smallest volume? Explain your answer.

   _____

   _____

Class Problem 1

Container D   **Container E**   **Container F**

Container D
holds 62 beans.
Container E
holds 43 beans.
Container F
holds 29 beans.

1. Which container has the largest volume?

_____

2. Which container would have the largest volume if you used water instead of beans?

_____

3. Suppose the beans from Container D are poured into empty Container F. Will all the beans fit? How could you find out how many beans from Container D will fit in Container F?

_____

_____

Class Problem 2

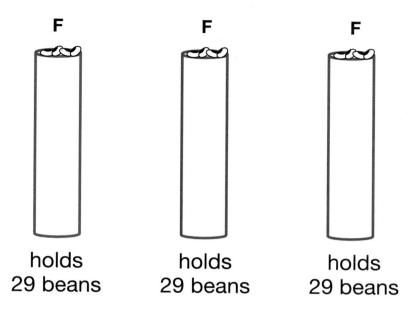

holds
29 beans

holds
29 beans

holds
29 beans

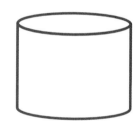

Container D
holds 62 beans.

Can an empty Container D hold all of the beans from the 3 filled F
containers? How can we find out?

_____

_____

_____

_____

UNIT 7

Sarah's Cube Models

Sarah made two cube models. Her plans are below.

Back

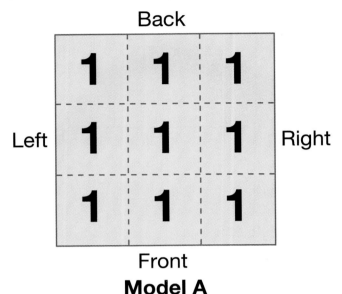

Left   Right

Front
Model A

Make Sarah's cube
models using her plans.

Which model do you
think is the biggest?
Explain why.

_____

_____

_____

_____

_____

_____

_____

_____

Back

Left   Right

Front
Model B

Sarah and Sebastian's
Cube Tower Plan

Sarah and Sebastian used cubes to make a tower.

Sebastian, let's draw a plan to build a tower.

Write two different number sentences that describe the volume in cubic units.

_____

_____

Back

4	**2**	**1**
2	**2**	**1**
1	**1**	**1**

Left   Right

Front

Galen's Cube Tower Plan

Use the plan below to build a tower that looks like the one Galen built.

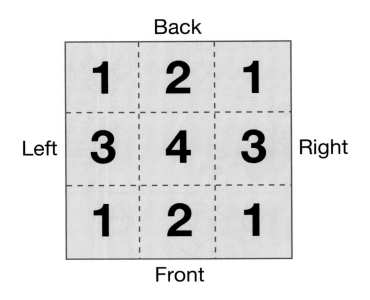

Back

Left   Right

1	2	1
3	4	3
1	2	1

Front

1. Ask your teacher to show you a model of Galen's tower. Does it look like yours?

_____

2. What is the volume of your tower?

_____

3. Write a number sentence to describe the volume in cubic units.

_____

_____

What If Volume Problems

H⊙m⊜w⊙rk

Below are the cube model plans you used to build two towers.

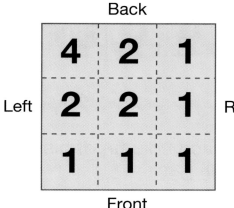

Back

Left ... Right

Front

Sarah and Sebastian's Cube Model Plan

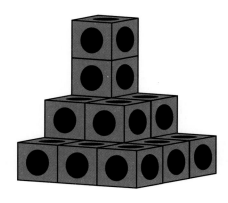

1. What is the volume of this model? _____

2. What if Sarah and Sebastian added one story to each column of their building? What will the new volume be?

   _____ Write a number sentence to describe

   the new volume in cubic units. _____

3. What if they made all the columns the same height as the tallest column? Write a number sentence to describe this

   volume in cubic units. _____

Copyright © 1997 by Kendall/Hunt Publishing Company

Homework

Below is Galen's Cube Model Plan.

Back

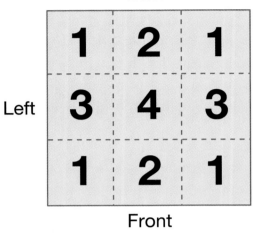

Left   Right

1	2	1
3	4	3
1	2	1

Front

Galen's Cube Model Plan

4. What is the volume of this model? _____

5. What if Galen added two stories to each column of his building? What would the new volume be?

_____ Write a number sentence to describe

the new volume in cubic units. _____

6. What if the center column of Galen's building was seven stories high instead of four stories high? Write a number sentence to describe this volume in cubic units.

_____

City Buildings

Use the drawings below to make three cube models. Find the volume of each building.

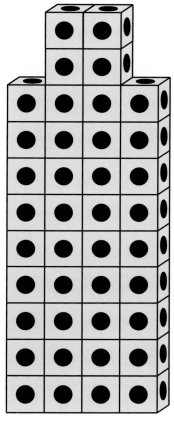

Quad City Towers

Volume _____

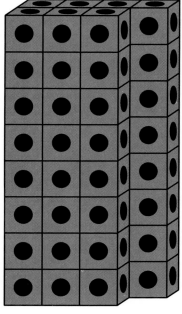

Six Corners Gym

Volume _____

Volume _____

Stair Step Apartments

City Buildings Match-Up

Which cube model goes with which cube plan? Draw a line from the plan to the matching model.

Plan 1

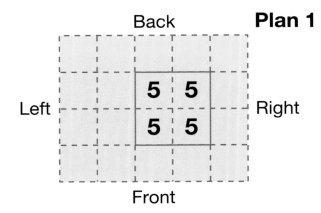

Back

Left

5	**5**
5	**5**

Right

Front

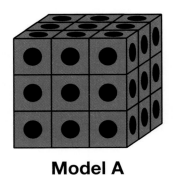

Model A

Plan 2

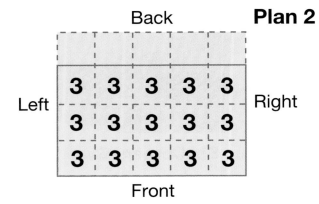

Back

Left

3	**3**	**3**	**3**	**3**
3	**3**	**3**	**3**	**3**
3	**3**	**3**	**3**	**3**

Right

Front

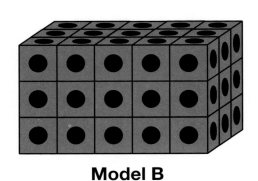

Model B

Plan 3

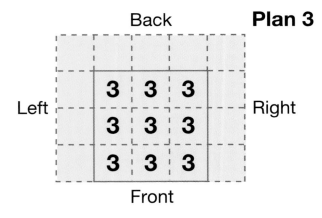

Back

Left

3	**3**	**3**
3	**3**	**3**
3	**3**	**3**

Right

Front

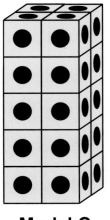

Model C

Cube Model Problems

1. Use the following floor plans to make a cube model building out of:

A. 9 cubes

Back

Left | | Right

Front

B. 11 cubes

Back

Left | | Right

Front

C. 16 cubes

Back

Left | | Right

Front

2. Use the following floor plan to make a building out of 9 cubes.

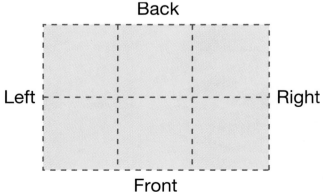

Back

Left | | Right

Front

UNIT 8

Millie, Minnie, Marty, and Mike Did It!

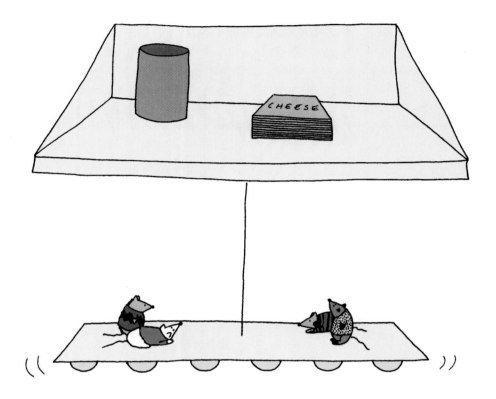

There are many possible combinations of masses for **Millie** and **Mike**, balancing **Minnie** and **Marty** on the hanging lamp. How many different combinations can you find?

Work with a partner. Pretend the mice can have any of these masses: 9 grams, 8 grams, 7 grams, 6 grams, 5 grams, 4 grams, 3 grams, 2 grams, or 1 gram. Each mouse has a different mass.

You can use connecting cubes to make each mouse's mass to check your combinations on the equal-arm balance.

Record the combinations of masses in the tables below. Millie's and Mike's total mass should equal Minnie's and Marty's total mass.

Mouse Masses in Grams

Millie	Mike	Total		Minnie	Marty	Total

Measuring Mass

Draw

Draw a picture of the lab. Include the two main variables and the materials you will use.

Before you collect data, what must you do to the balance?

_____

Measuring Mass

Measuring Mass Data Table

Collect

Find any object that is approximately 100 grams and 4 small objects to mass. Both partners should find each *M* on their own and then check each other's results.

O Objects	*M* Mass (in _____) *unit*

Graph

Make a bar graph of the data. Label both axes.

Explore

1. **A.** Which of your objects has the least mass?

   _____

   B. If you had four of these objects, would their combined mass be more than 100 grams or less than 100 grams?

   _____

   How did you figure it out?

   _____

   _____

   _____

2. **A.** Which of your objects has the most mass?

   _____

   B. Would three 40-gram objects have more mass or less mass than your heaviest object?

   _____

   How did you figure it out?

   _____

   _____

Measuring Mass

3. A. Find the sum of the masses of your heaviest object and your lightest object.

_____

B. Put these two objects in one balance pan and mass them. Did you get the same answer as in Question 3A? Why or why not?

_____

_____

_____

1	heaviest object		lightest objects

4. How many of your lighter objects come closest to balancing your heaviest object? How do you know?

_____

_____

_____

UNIT 9

Numbers and Sense

Solve the following problems by estimating the sum. Each time, tell how you made your estimate.

1. Katen and Arlene added the caps in Sections A–D. Arlene counted 27 caps in Section A and 14 caps in Section B. Katen counted 32 caps in Section C and 48 caps in Section D. Estimate the number of caps in Sections A–D.

   _____

   _____

2. The hot dog vendor sold 68 hot dogs with ketchup, 12 hot dogs with mustard, and 9 plain hot dogs. Estimate the number of hot dogs sold.

   _____

   _____

3. The Chicago Cubs and the Chicago White Sox played a doubleheader. The Cubs had 22 hits in the first game and 13 hits in the second. The White Sox had 28 hits in the first game and 17 hits in the second. Estimate the number of hits in all.

   _____

   _____

Computer Game Seminar

The Compute with Us Game Company held a seminar for school children. The students discussed new computer games. Help the secretary total the data collected at the seminar for the annual report. Explain your thinking for each problem.

1. Twenty-nine students were from Chicago, Illinois, and thirty-three students were from Springfield, Illinois. How many students came from Illinois?

_____

_____

_____

2. In the morning session, the students named their favorite type of computer game. Fifty-five students liked sports games. Thirty-eight students liked space games. How many students were in the morning session?

_____

_____

_____

3. In the afternoon session, 54 students reported that space games were their favorite, 27 liked adventure games, and 32 liked sports games. Did more or less than 100 students attend the afternoon session?

_____

_____

_____

4. In the morning session, 46 students drew new characters they would like to see in a game. In the afternoon session, 36 students drew new characters. How many students drew new characters?

_____

_____

_____

5. Pretend you were the secretary at the seminar. What did you find out? Write a problem and find the answer.

_____

_____

_____

An Addition Seminar

How Did They Do It?

Pretend you are a teacher, checking to see how your students solved this problem:

$$\begin{array}{r} 26 \\ + 58 \\ \hline \end{array}$$

Shanila showed her work like this:

$$\begin{array}{r} 26 \\ +58 \\ \hline 84 \end{array}$$ ~~||||~~ ~~||||~~ ~~||||~~ ~~||||~~ ~~||||~~ |

~~||||~~ ~~||||~~ ~~||||~~ ~~||||~~ ~~||||~~ ~~||||~~ ~~||||~~ ~~||||~~ ~~||||~~ ~~||||~~ ~~||||~~ |||

What did she do to solve the problem?

Devon used the 200 chart and showed his work like this:

$$\begin{array}{r} 26 \\ +58 \\ \hline 84 \end{array}$$

26	36	46	56	66	76

77	78	79	80	81	82	83	84

What did he do?

Show another way to solve the problem.

Building Addition Problems

Before you do the problems below, estimate the answer. After you solve each problem, explain how to do the problem two different ways.

1. The sum will be between _____ and _____.

$$
\begin{array}{r}
24 \\
+\ 58 \\
\hline
\end{array}
$$

2. The sum will be between _____ and _____.

$$
\begin{array}{r}
65 \\
+\ 26 \\
\hline
\end{array}
$$

3. The sum will be between _____ and _____.

$$
\begin{array}{r}
27 \\
13 \\
+\ 55 \\
\hline
\end{array}
$$

Exploring with Base-ten Pieces

What Happened Here?

Michael completed the following problem:

$$\begin{array}{r} 48 \\ + 49 \\ \hline 817 \end{array}$$

1. Is this a reasonable answer for this problem? How do you know?

_____

_____

2. What do you think Michael might have done?

_____

_____

3. How would you solve this problem? Make sure you explain your thinking.

_____

_____

Adding Two Ways

Homework

Solve the problem two ways. Show your thinking.

---

1. First way:

   42
   + 49
   _____

---

2. Second way:

   42
   + 49
   _____

Adding with Paper and Pencil

Think It Through

Homework

Solve the following problems using paper-and-pencil addition. Show your thinking.

1. Jeremiah and Jordan collect baseball cards. Jeremiah has 56 Chicago White Sox cards. Jordan has 48 Chicago Cubs cards. If they combine their collections, how many Chicago cards will they have?

2. For his birthday, Jeremiah received 26 more White Sox cards to go with the 56 he already had. How many White Sox cards are now in his collection?

3. Jordan decided to collect Cardinal cards as well. He bought 35 cards to add to his collection of 48 cards. How many cards are now in his collection?

4.
$$\begin{array}{r} 25 \\ +\ 26 \\ \hline \end{array}$$

5.
$$\begin{array}{r} 68 \\ +\ 23 \\ \hline \end{array}$$

6.
$$\begin{array}{r} 45 \\ +\ 48 \\ \hline \end{array}$$

Shooting Star Snack Shop
Children's Menu

Food

Pizza Slice....................................	79¢
Taco..	59¢
Grilled Cheese Sandwich............	89¢
Turkey Sandwich.........................	99¢
Peanut Butter and Crackers........	49¢
Bagel..	29¢
Potato Chips...............................	25¢
Pretzels......................................	25¢
Brownie......................................	35¢
Fruit Salad Cup...........................	65¢
Carrot Sticks...............................	29¢
Chicken Noodle Soup..................	55¢
Chili...	75¢

Drinks	Small	Medium	Large
Milk...............................	25¢	40¢	55¢
Lemonade.....................	39¢	55¢	79¢
Orange Juice.................	55¢	70¢	85¢
Hot Chocolate...............	59¢	75¢	99¢

Snack Shop Addition

Snack Shop Bills

Shooting Star Snack Shop
You have up to $5.00 to spend.

Customer's Name:

Enrique

Item	Price(¢)
Grilled Cheese	89¢
Carrot Sticks	29¢
Chicken Noodle Soup	55¢
Brownie	35¢
Milk	55¢

Total is between

_____ and _____   Total _____

Is your total reasonable?

_____

Shooting Star Snack Shop

Customer's Name:

_____

Item	Price(¢)
_____	_____
_____	_____
_____	_____
_____	_____
_____	_____

Total is between

_____ and _____   Total _____

Is your total reasonable?

_____

Shooting Star Snack Shop
You have up to $2.00 to spend.

Item	Price(¢)
_____	_____
_____	_____
_____	_____
_____	_____

Customer's Name:

_____

Is your total reasonable?

Total _____ _____

Total is between

_____ and _____

Shooting Star Snack Shop
You have up to $3.50 to spend.

Item	Price(¢)
_____	_____
_____	_____
_____	_____
_____	_____

Customer's Name:

_____

Is your total reasonable?

Total _____ _____

Total is between

_____ and _____

Snack Shop Addition

Oops, I Spilled the Juice!

Splash the Spiller and his friend, Nick, bought lunch at the Shooting Star Snack Shop. Unfortunately, Splash spilled juice on their bills so the prices of the specials, the homemade applesauce and banana bread, are blotted out.

Shooting Star Snack Shop Bill	
Customer's Name	_Splash_
Item	Price (¢)
Fruit Salad Cup	65¢
Pretzels	25¢
Cup of Applesauce	▮
Orange Juice	85¢
Total	$2.04

Shooting Star Snack Shop Bill	
Customer's Name	_Nick_
Item	Price (¢)
Chili	75¢
Taco	59¢
Banana Bread	▮
Medium Milk	40¢
Total	$2.23

How much did the applesauce cost?

How much did the banana bread cost?

Snack Shop Carryout

Homework

Make up your own problem on the bill below using your menu. If you ask family members or friends to place orders, you may use the space provided to list more items. Describe how you found your answer.

Shooting Star Snack Shop

Customer's Name:

_____

Item	Price(¢)
_____	_____
_____	_____
_____	_____
_____	_____
_____	_____

Total is between

Is your total reasonable?

_____ and _____   Total _____   _____

Use your menu to complete each bill. You may find the total any way you choose, including the use of a calculator.

Shooting Star Snack Shop

Item	Price(¢)	Customer's Name:
Grilled Cheese	_____	_____
Potato Chips	_____	
Fruit Salad Cup	_____	
_____	_____	
_____	_____	Is your total reasonable?

Total is between

_____ and _____   Total _____   _____

Shooting Star Snack Shop

Item	Price(¢)	Customer's Name:
Pizza Slice	_____	_____
Carrot Sticks	_____	
Lemonade	_____	
_____	_____	
_____	_____	Is your total reasonable?

Total is between

_____ and _____   Total _____   _____

100
90
80
70
60
50
40
30
20
10
cc

Scales Worksheet 1

Look at the scale to the right.

Write the number for each letter.

A. _____

B. _____

C. _____

D. _____

E. _____

F. _____

Make an arrow at 85, and mark it "G."

Make an arrow at 97, and mark it "H."

```
                         ─── 100
                         ═
                         ═
                         ─── 90
                         ═
                         ═
                         ─── 80
                         ═
              F  ──→     ═
                         ─── 70
                         ═
                         ═
                         ─── 60
              E  ──→     ═
                         ═
                         ─── 50
              D  ──→     ═
                         ═
                         ─── 40
              C  ──→     ═
                         ═
                         ─── 30
                         ═
              B  ──→     ═
                         ─── 20
                         ═
                         ═
                         ─── 10
              A  ──→     ═
                         ═
                         ─── 0
```

Scales Worksheet 2

Look at the scale to the right.

Write the number for each letter.

A. _____

B. _____

C. _____

D. _____

E. _____

F. _____

Make an arrow at 110, and mark it "G."

Make an arrow at 119, and mark it "H."

Scales Worksheet 3

For problems 1 and 2, write the temperature the thermometer shows.

For problem 3, color the thermometer to show 85°. For problem 4, show 103°.

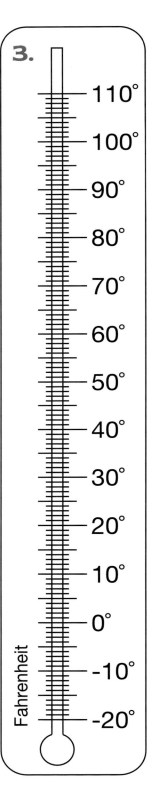

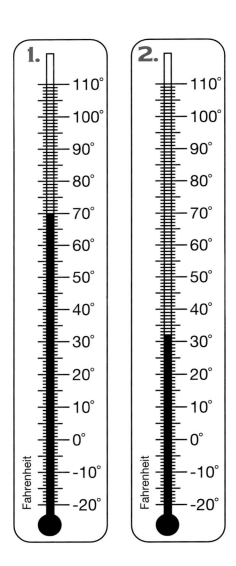

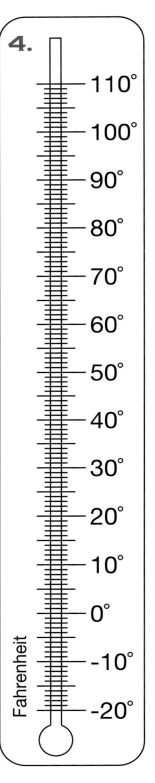

Scales Worksheet 4

For problems 1 and 2, write the speed that each speedometer shows.

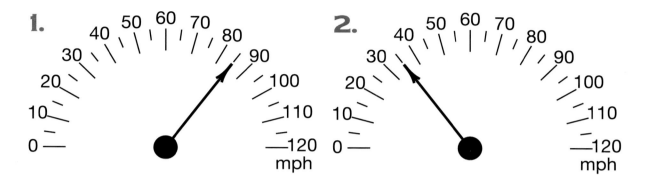

1.

_____

2.

_____

For problems 3 and 4, draw an arrow to show the speed on each speedometer.

3.

80 mph

4.

55 mph

Understanding Scales

Look at the scale to the right.

Write the number for each letter.

A. _____

B. _____

C. _____

D. _____

E. _____

F. _____

Make an arrow at 62, and mark it "G."

Make an arrow at 75, and mark it "H."

```
                    ─── 80
                    ───
                    ───
                    ─── 70
                    ───
                    ───
                    ─── 60
                    ───
         F ──→      ───
                    ─── 50
         E ──→      ───
         D ──→      ─── 40
                    ───
                    ───
                    ─── 30
         C ──→      ───
                    ───
         B ──→      ─── 20
                    ───
                    ───
                    ─── 10
         A ──→      ───
                    ───
                    ─── 0
```

Reading Graduated Cylinders

Collect

Work with a partner to read the graduated cylinders your teacher has put out.

Cylinder	V Volume in _____ unit		
	Partner 1	**Partner 2**	**Agreed Reading**

Filling Graduated Cylinders

Work with a partner to fill and read water levels in graduated cylinders.

Materials

- beaker filled with water
- eyedropper
- graduated cylinder
- paper towels (to clean up spills)

The eyedropper helps you get exact volumes.

Directions

1. One partner should put some water in the graduated cylinder. The dropper can be used to add just a little extra water.

2. The other partner should read the volume and write it down.

3. The first partner should check the reading and write it down.

4. Both partners must agree on the reading and record it.

5. After both partners agree, pour the water back into the beaker.

6. Repeat the process by taking turns putting water in the cylinder and reading it.

First Partner's Reading	Second Partner's Reading	Agreed Reading

How to Fill a Graduated Cylinder

Explain how to fill a graduated cylinder correctly. Use clue words like *first, next,* and *finally* to tell the steps in order.

_____

_____

_____

_____

_____

Draw

Draw a picture showing how to fill a graduated cylinder.

Remember to show the scale.

Measuring Volume

Draw

Draw a picture of the lab setup.

Collect

Fill a graduated cylinder with 80 cc of water. Pick at least four objects, including a chain of centimeter connecting cubes. Fill in the data table.

Measuring Volume Data Table 1

Object	V (Water) in _____ unit	V (Total) in _____ unit	V (Object) in _____ unit

Graph

Make a bar graph of your data on a piece of bar graph paper.

Explore

Work together to answer the following questions.

1. Which object has the most volume? What is its volume?

_____

_____

2. Which object has the least volume? What is its volume?

_____

_____

3. What is the difference in volume between the two objects? Show how you found your answer.

_____

4. Look at Measuring Volume Data Table 1. Find the volume of three times the number of objects listed in the first column. If the water level is at 80 cc, which objects will overflow the 100 cc mark on the graduated cylinder?

Use Measuring Volume Data Table 2 to write your answers.

Measuring Volume Data Table 2

Object	V (Object) in _____ *unit*	V (triple) in _____ *unit*	Overflow 100 cc mark (Yes or No)

Volume Math Check

What is the volume of the clay in the cylinder labeled "after"?
Write a number sentence to show how you got your answer.

_____

_____

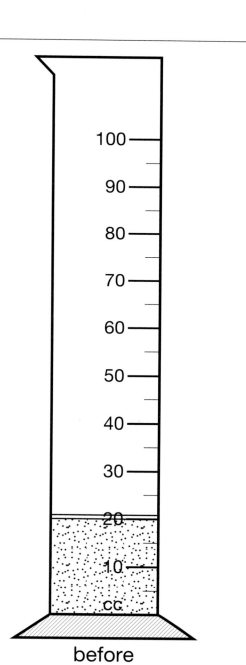

before

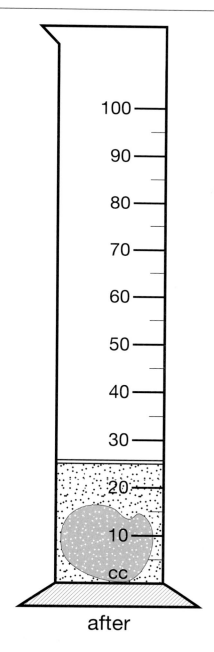

after

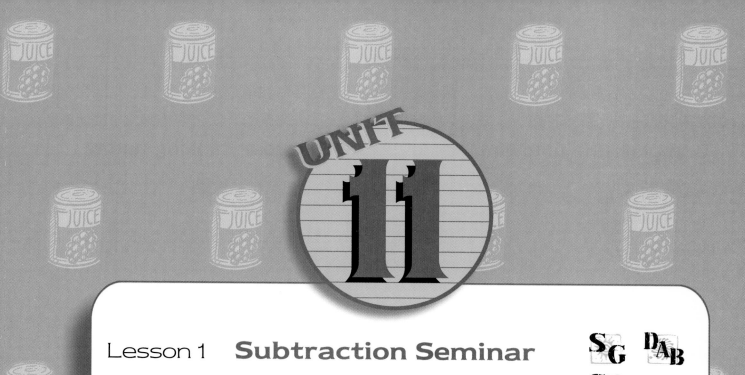

UNIT 11

More Thinking about Subtraction

Complete the following sentences. Show your thinking below.

1.

I know that my change is _____ ¢ because

2.

I know that the soup costs _____ ¢ more than the noodles because

3.

I know I need _____ more cents to buy the juice because

Which Answer Makes Sense?

Look at each problem. Decide which number is the best estimate of the correct answer. Explain why you think so in the space below the problem.

1. $\begin{array}{r} 60 \\ -27 \\ \hline \end{array}$ 45   30   50

2. $\begin{array}{r} 50 \\ -18 \\ \hline \end{array}$ 30   40   15

3. $\begin{array}{r} 50 \\ +22 \\ \hline \end{array}$ 30   70   20

4. $\begin{array}{r} 94 \\ -38 \\ \hline \end{array}$ 50   40   75

5. $\begin{array}{r} 71 \\ -34 \\ \hline \end{array}$ 40   50   60

Base-Ten Subtraction

Before you do a problem, estimate the answer. Show how to do the problem with base-ten pieces and one other way.

1. The difference will be between _____ and _____.

$$\begin{array}{r} 78 \\ -\ 25 \\ \hline \end{array}$$

with base-ten pieces	another way

2. The difference will be between _____ and _____.

$$\begin{array}{r} 84 \\ -\ 55 \\ \hline \end{array}$$

with base-ten pieces	another way

Base-Ten Subtraction

Ways to Subtract

Before you do a problem, estimate the answer. Show how to do the problem with base-ten pieces and one other way.

1. The difference will be between _____ and _____.

$$\begin{array}{r} 41 \\ -\ 29 \\ \hline \end{array}$$

with base-ten pieces	another way

2. The difference will be between _____ and _____.

$$\begin{array}{r} 63 \\ -\ 27 \\ \hline \end{array}$$

with base-ten pieces	another way

More Baseball Cards

Solve the following problems. Draw a picture or write to explain your thinking.

1. Jeremiah has 56 White Sox baseball cards. Jordan has 28. How many more cards does Jeremiah have than Jordan?

2. Jeremiah's mom started collecting baseball cards when she was 8 years old. She is now 44. How many years has she collected cards?

3. Jordan had 34 Cardinal cards. He sold 18 to a friend. How many Cardinal cards does he have left?

4. Jeremiah has 26 Yankee cards, 36 Red Sox cards, and 19 Cardinal cards in his drawer. How many cards are in his drawer?

5.
$$\begin{array}{r} 50 \\ -32 \\ \hline \end{array}$$

6.
$$\begin{array}{r} 73 \\ -42 \\ \hline \end{array}$$

7.
$$\begin{array}{r} 25 \\ +48 \\ \hline \end{array}$$

8.
$$\begin{array}{r} 61 \\ -38 \\ \hline \end{array}$$

Many Ways to Find the Answer

Solve the problem three different ways.

1. First way:

Problem

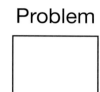

2. Second way:

3. Third way:

Shooting Star Snack Shop
Children's Menu

Food

Pizza Slice....................................	79¢
Taco...	59¢
Grilled Cheese Sandwich............	89¢
Turkey Sandwich........................	99¢
Peanut Butter and Crackers........	49¢
Bagel...	29¢
Potato Chips..............................	25¢
Pretzels.......................................	25¢
Brownie.......................................	35¢
Fruit Salad Cup...........................	65¢
Carrot Sticks...............................	29¢
Chicken Noodle Soup.................	55¢
Chili...	75¢

Drinks	Small	Medium	Large
Milk..............................	25¢	40¢	55¢
Lemonade....................	39¢	55¢	79¢
Orange Juice................	55¢	70¢	85¢
Hot Chocolate..............	59¢	75¢	99¢

Snack Shop Bills 2

You have $1.75. Do you have enough money to buy the items listed below?	You have 40¢. Do you have enough money to buy the items listed below?
Estimate: yes _____ no _____	**Estimate:** yes _____ no _____
Actual:	**Actual:**
Peanut Butter and Crackers _____	Bagel _____
Chicken Noodle Soup _____	Pretzels _____
Small Milk _____	
Total _____	**Total** _____
How much more money do you need? _____	How much more money do you need? _____
or	or
How much change will you get? _____	How much change will you get? _____

You have 80¢. Do you have enough money to buy the items listed below?

Estimate: yes _____ no _____

Actual:

Chicken Noodle
Soup   _____

Carrot Sticks   _____

Total   _____

How much more money do

you need? _____

or

How much change will you

get? _____

You have 94¢. Do you have enough money to buy the items listed below?

Estimate: yes _____ no _____

Actual:

Taco   _____

Brownie   _____

Small Milk   _____

Total   _____

How much more money do

you need? _____

or

How much change will you

get? _____

Snack Shop Addition and Subtraction

Choose items from the menu to complete the bill below. Find the amount of change you should receive. Show how you solved the problem in the space provided.

Shooting Star Snack Shop
You have up to $1.50 to spend.

Item	Price(¢)	Customer's Name:
_____	_____	_____
_____	_____	
_____	_____	
_____	_____	
_____	_____	Change due
Total	_____	_____

Snack Shop Carryout 2

Homework

Use the Shooting Star Snack Shop Children's Menu to complete the following. You may solve the problems any way you choose, including the use of a calculator.

You have 68¢. Do you have enough money to buy the items listed below?	You have 95¢. Do you have enough money to buy the items listed below?
Estimate: yes _____ no _____	**Estimate:** yes _____ no _____
Actual:	**Actual:**
Bagel _____	Pizza Slice _____
Small Milk _____	Carrot Sticks _____
Total _____	**Total** _____
How much more money do you need? _____	How much more money do you need? _____
or	or
How much change will you get? _____	How much change will you get? _____

Snack Shop Addition and Subtraction

Choose items from the menu to complete the bill below. Find the amount of change you should receive. Show how you solved the problem in the space provided.

Shooting Star Snack Shop
You have up to $2.50 to spend.

Item	Price(¢)	Customer's Name:
		_____
_____	_____	
_____	_____	
_____	_____	
_____	_____	
_____	_____	Change due
Total	_____	_____

UNIT 12

135

Children's Zoo Produce

Help the zookeeper order food for a three-day weekend. The first order slip shows how much food the zoo needs for one day.

1.

Order Slip

13 Stalks of Celery

For One Day

Order Slip

_____ **Stalks of Celery**

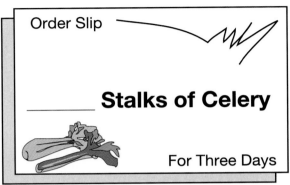

For Three Days

2.

Order Slip

12 Bags of Apples

For One Day

Order Slip

_____ **Bags of Apples**

For Three Days

3.

Order Slip

17 Heads of Lettuce

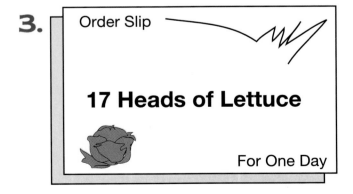

For One Day

Order Slip

_____ **Heads of Lettuce**

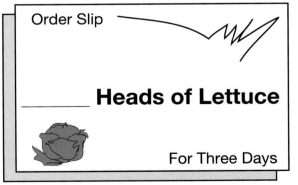

For Three Days

In the Zoo Kitchen

Name _____ **Date** _____

4.

Order Slip

15 Bags of Peanuts

For One Day

Order Slip

_____ **Bags of Peanuts**

For Three Days

5.

Order Slip

16 Bunches of Grapes

For One Day

Order Slip

_____ **Bunches of Grapes**

For Three Days

6.

Order Slip

7 Bags of Spinach

For One Day

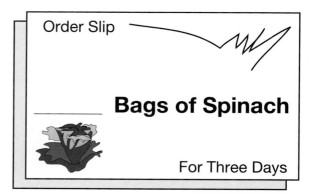

Order Slip

_____ **Bags of Spinach**

For Three Days

Name _____   Date _____

Great Ape House

Help the zookeeper share food for the 5 ape families. The first delivery slip shows how much food the zoo has.

1.

Delivery Slip

30 Stalks of Celery

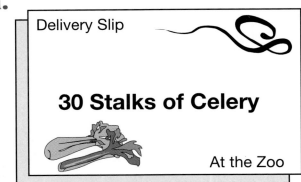

At the Zoo

Delivery Slip

_____ **Stalks of Celery**

Per Ape Family

2.

Delivery Slip

25 Bags of Apples

At the Zoo

Delivery Slip

_____ **Bags of Apples**

Per Ape Family

3.

Delivery Slip

22 Heads of Lettuce

At the Zoo

Delivery Slip

_____ **Heads of Lettuce**

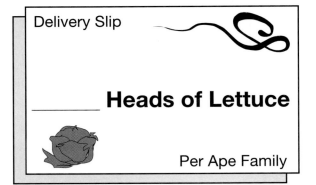

Per Ape Family

In the Zoo Kitchen

4.

Delivery Slip

40 Melons

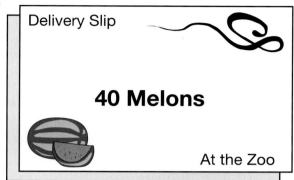

At the Zoo

Delivery Slip

_____ **Melons**

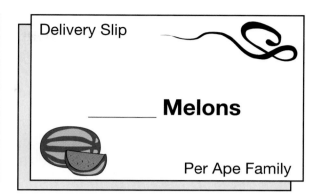

Per Ape Family

5.

Delivery Slip

27 Boxes of Pears

At the Zoo

Delivery Slip

_____ **Boxes of Pears**

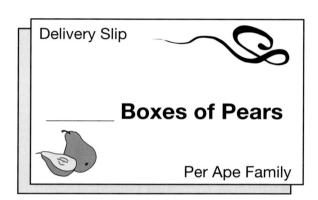

Per Ape Family

6.

Delivery Slip

8 Bags of Onions

At the Zoo

Delivery Slip

_____ **Bags of Onions**

Per Ape Family

Zoo Kitchen Problems

Draw pictures and write number sentences to solve the following problems.

1. Marcus fed 4 rabbits, 2 heads of lettuce each. How many

heads of lettuce did Marcus use? _____

2. Kristie works with horses. She feeds the horses 6 bales of hay each day. How many bales of hay does Kristie need for

a three-day weekend? _____

3. Jessica has ten apples that she wants to share with the monkeys. If there are four monkeys in the pen, how many

apples can each monkey have? _____

How Many?

Homework

Draw a picture for each problem. Then, write a number sentence to answer the question.

1. Draw 6 monkey faces.

How many eyes are there in all? _____

---

2. Draw 3 zoo cars.

How many tires are there in all? _____

3. Draw 4 zoo tricycles.

How many wheels are there in all? _____

_____

4. Draw your own picture about equal groups.

How many _____ are there in all? _____

Zoo Problems

Use drawings to solve Questions 1–3. Write a number sentence to show how you solved the problem.

1. Jerry had 4 apples and 3 bananas. How many pieces of fruit

did he have? _____

2. There were 4 monkeys. Each monkey had 3 bananas. How

many bananas were there altogether? _____

3. There were 4 sea lions, 3 polar bears, and 3 seals in the
pool. What is the total number of animals in the pool?

_____

Zoo Stickers

Mario, Jacob, and Lisa each bought a sheet of stickers at the zoo. How many stickers did each student buy? Write a number sentence to show your answer.

Mario

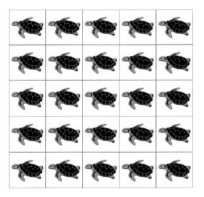

Jacob

Lisa

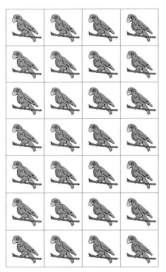

_____

_____   _____

Zoo Stickers and Stamps

Name _____ Date _____

Zoo Stamps

Mary Beth, Tony, and Shana each bought a page of zoo stamps. Write a number sentence to show how you found the answers to the questions below.

Mary Beth

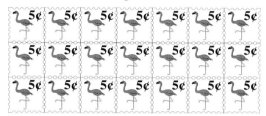

1. How many stamps?

_____

2. How much did all of her stamps cost?

_____

Tony

3. How many stamps?

_____

4. Total cost? _____

Shana

5. How many stamps?

_____

6. Total cost? _____

Lunchtime at the Bird House

It is lunchtime at the Bird House. Help the zookeeper share the food. Draw pictures and write a number sentence to show how many each bird will get.

1. Draw 6 bird bowls. Share 18 orange segments.

How many will each bird get? _____

_____

2. Draw 3 bird bowls. Share 12 grapes.

How many will each bird get? _____

3. Draw 4 bird bowls. Share 9 leaves of spinach.

How many will each bird get? _____

4. Draw your own number of bird bowls. Share 12 bananas.

How many will each bird get? _____

Fruits and Vegetables
for the Reptile House

Shipments	Daily Amount Needed	Number of Days Food Will Last
10 bags of zucchini	2 bags	
25 bags of apples	5 bags	
17 bunches of carrots	4 bunches	
12 bags of kale	3 bags	
14 bags of beans	2 bags	
11 bags of escarole	2 bags	

A Problem I Saw

Homework

What did you see on your way home from school today? Use some of these things to write a multiplication or a division problem for the rest of your class to solve. Draw a picture to show what you are multiplying or dividing.

UNIT 13

Classifying and Sorting Lids

Using your sample of lids, what do you want to find out about your sample? I want to find out

_____

_____

Draw a picture. Show how you will sort the lids. Show the variable and its values.

Lids Data Table

Collect

Sort the lids in your sample. Record the data below.

Lids

	N Number

Graph

Make a bar graph of your data on graph paper.

Explore

What does the graph show you about the lids in your sample? Write about it.

_____

_____

Frank and Kaley's Lids

Frank and Kaley wanted to study the material and color of their lids. They made two data tables.

Lid Material

M Material	N Number
plastic	57
metal	33

Lid Color

C Color	N Number
white	11
red	5
blue	23
silver	17
gold	24
other	10

Use the tables to answer the questions.

1. What is the most common color? _____

2. How many lids are there altogether? How did you find your

answer? _____

_____

3. What is another way to find out how many lids there are?

_____

_____

4. Can you tell how many of the plastic lids are red?

Explain. _____

_____

Frank and Kaley want to compare the color of metal lids and plastic lids. Discuss with your partner or group some other ways that Frank and Kaley could make data tables for their study. Show your new data table(s) below.

Undercover Investigation

Purpose: My class wants to find out _____

_____

Draw ⟍⟋⟍⟋⟍⟍⟍⟍⟍⟍⟍⟍⟍⟍⟍⟍⟍

Draw a picture. Show the two variables and their values.

Collect

What data tables will you need? Decide with your class.

Graph

What bar graphs will you make? Decide with your class. Make your graphs on separate sheets of graph paper.

Discuss

1. What does your class data tell you about the lids that people usually throw away?

_____

_____

_____

_____

2. Compare your class results to the data you and your partner collected. Is the data similar?

_____

_____

Mena Sorts for Recycling

Mena collects lids to be recycled. She sorts them by color and material. Here is the data table she made for this week. Use her data to answer the questions.

M Material	*C* Color		
	Gold	Black	White
metal	7	2	3
plastic	14	7	20

1. A. Are there more black lids or white lids?

_____

B. How many more?

_____

2. A. Are there more gold lids or white lids?

_____

B. How many more?

_____

3. Which color has the greatest number of lids?

_____

4. Which color has the fewest number of lids?

_____

5. A. Are there more plastic lids or metal lids?

_____

B. How many more?

_____

C. Is it more than twice as many more?

_____

6. Mena collected twice as many lids last week. Estimate the number of plastic lids that she collected last week. Explain how you got that number.

_____

_____

_____

_____

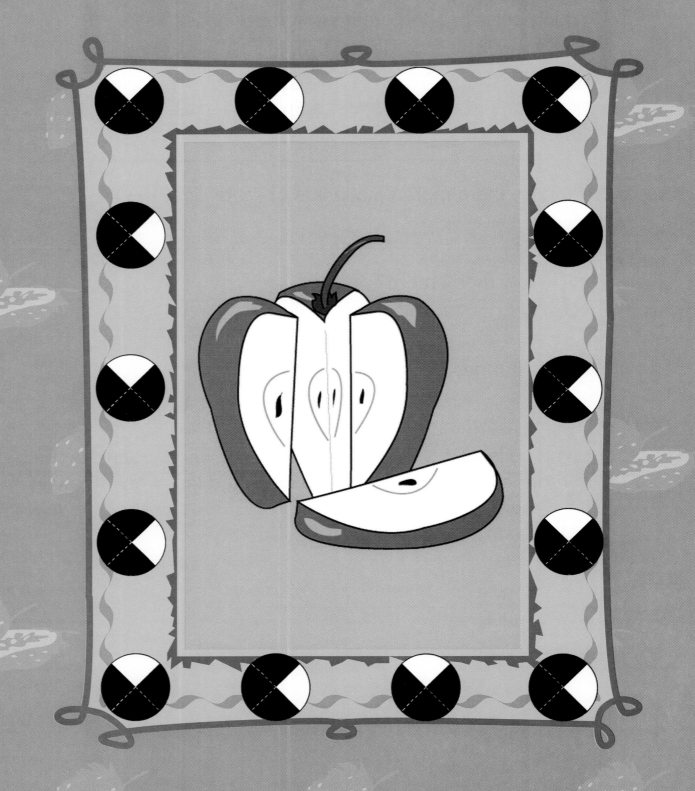

UNIT 14

Banana Split

After buying a banana at a local fruit store,
Jes and Bes started squabbling about who would get more.

"Let's cut it in half," said the first to the other.
"We'll each have two pieces and none for our brother."

"Hold on one minute!" the second one cried.
"I think we'll get more if we further divide.

Halves means two pieces. In fourths, there are four.
If we split the fruit that way, we're bound to get more!"

"But if fourths are good, then eighths must be great!"
So, they both got four pieces, which each of them ate.

**Do Jes and Bes understand fractions?
Explain. You may wish to draw a picture
to help explain your thinking.**

_____

_____

_____

_____

Folding Fractions

Tile Fractions 1

Follow the directions for covering each shape with tiles. Then, remove the tiles, and color each shape to show how you covered it.

1. one-half red and one-half green

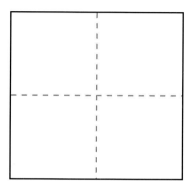

2. one-third blue and two-thirds yellow

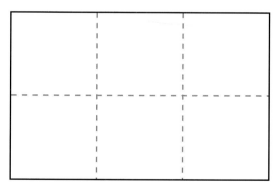

3. one-fourth red and three-fourths blue

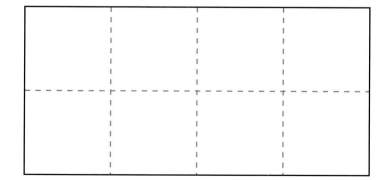

Tile Fractions 2

Continue working as you did in *Tile Fractions 1*.

1. one-fourth red, one-fourth yellow, and one-half green

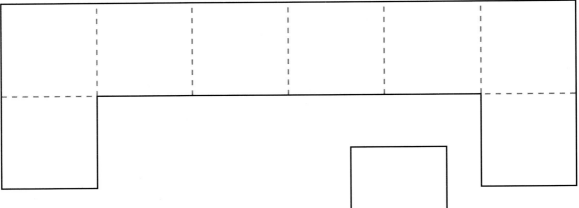

2. one-half yellow and one-half blue

3. one-third blue and two-thirds yellow

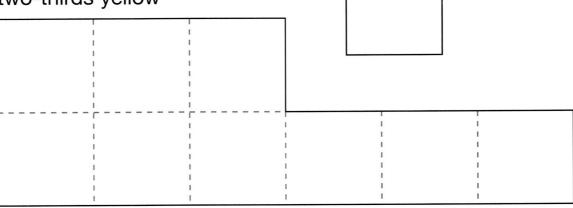

Tile Fractions

Tile Fractions 3

Follow the directions for covering each shape with tiles. Then, remove the tiles, and color each shape to show how you covered it.

1. one-half green and one-half yellow

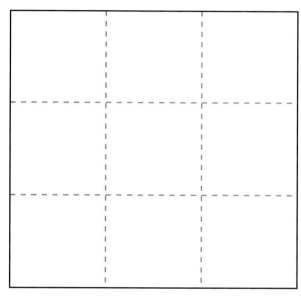

2. Use your color tiles to make your own shape one-half blue and one-half green. Then, draw and color your shape on the dots below.

· · · · · ·

· · · · · ·

· · · · · ·

More Tile Fractions

Homework

1. Color one-third green
    and two-thirds yellow.

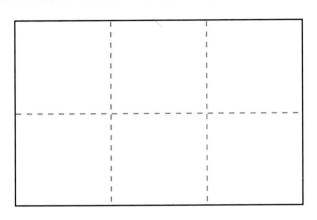

2. Show how you would draw and color a shape that is
    covered with square-inch tiles one-half blue and one-half
    yellow.

·   ·   ·   ·   ·   ·   ·

·   ·   ·   ·   ·   ·   ·

·   ·   ·   ·   ·   ·   ·

·   ·   ·   ·   ·   ·   ·

·   ·   ·   ·   ·   ·   ·

Tile Fractions

Fraction Games

Homework

Fraction War		Fraction Concentration	
Tally for Each Person	**Tally for Each 5 Minutes**	**Tally for Each Person**	**Tally for Each 5 Minutes**

Family member's signature _____

Child's signature _____

Return this sheet to school by _____

Rules

Fraction War (2 Players)

1. One player deals out all the cards, half to each player.
2. Each player lays his or her stack face down in a pile.
3. Each player turns over one card.
4. The player with the larger fraction takes both cards.
5. If the fractions are the same size, it is a war!
6. For a war, each player puts a second card face down and a third face up.
7. The player whose third card represents the larger fraction takes all the cards.
8. Cards that are won are added to the bottom of the player's pile.
9. Play for 10 minutes or until one player runs out of cards.
10. The player with the most cards at the end of the game wins.

Fraction Concentration (2 or More Players)

1. Players lay out all the cards face down in a big rectangle.
2. The first player turns over any two cards.
3. If the cards match, the player picks them up and takes another turn.
4. If the cards do not match, the player turns them face down, and the next player takes a turn.
5. The player with the most cards at the end wins.

Fraction Games

How Are All These Alike?

Tell how each fraction is like the other.

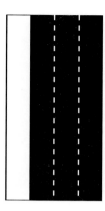

three-fourths
$\frac{3}{4}$

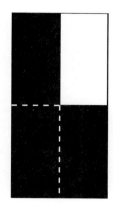

_____

_____

one-fourth
$\frac{1}{4}$

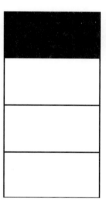

_____

_____

_____

UNIT 15

Shapes Grid

Use *yes* or *no* to answer each question on the grid.

Pattern Block Shape	Are opposite sides parallel?	Are opposite sides equal length?	Are all the sides of equal length?	How many sides are there?	Do all the corners look the same?
hexagon ⬡					
trapezoid ◤					
triangle ▶					
square ▮					
blue rhombus ▰					
tan rhombus ▱					

What Shape Am I?

Homework

Use the *Shapes Grid* you completed to solve the riddles.

1. I have four sides. They are all the same length.
What shape(s) can I be?

_____

2. My four sides are the same length. I also have square
corners. What shape(s) can I be?

_____

3. Two of my sides are parallel to one another. The other two
sides are not. What shape(s) can I be?

_____

4. All of my sides are the same length and all my corners look
the same too. What shape(s) can I be?

_____

5. Two of the triangle pattern blocks can be put together to
form me. What shape(s) can I be?

_____

6. Write your own riddle. Give it to a friend to solve.

_____

_____

Name _____   Date _____

Professor Peabody Visits Flatville

Professor Peabody is visiting Flatville. Everything in Flatville is two-dimensional or flat, even the people! They are called Flatniks. The first person Professor Peabody met was a scientist named Professor Ima Rectangle.

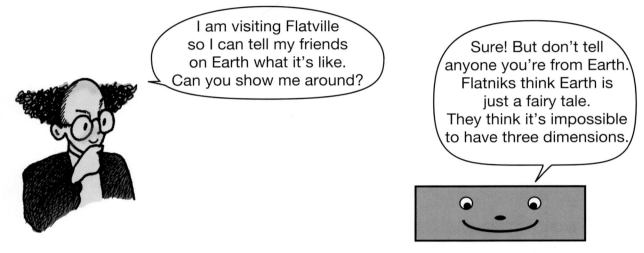

I am visiting Flatville so I can tell my friends on Earth what it's like. Can you show me around?

Sure! But don't tell anyone you're from Earth. Flatniks think Earth is just a fairy tale. They think it's impossible to have three dimensions.

People in Flatville have three ways of moving around. One way is called **sliding**. Watch what happens if Professor Rectangle slides east.

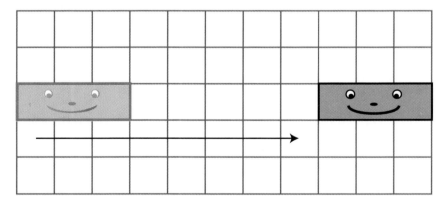

N
W ← → E
S

Professor Peabody Visits Flatville

Name _____   Date _____

Another way of moving is called **turning**. Tell how Professor Rectangle moved to get into the library.

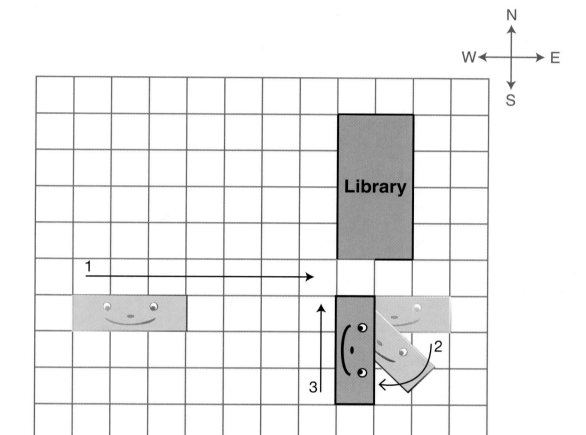

_____

_____

_____

_____

Professor Rectangle bought a car and tried to park it in her garage by moving with slides and turns, but it would not fit. Try it! Use slides and turns to park Professor Rectangle's car in her garage.

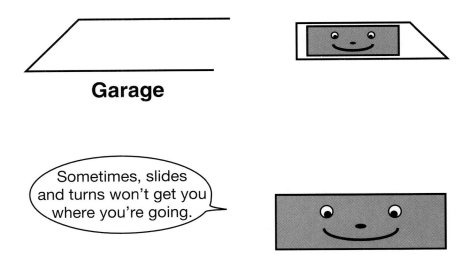

Garage

Professor Rectangle has to use a machine called the Flip-O-Tron to get into her garage. Pressing the Flip-O-Tron button causes an object in Flatville to get **flipped**. Notice what happened to Professor Rectangle's car after it was flipped. Now it fits in her garage.

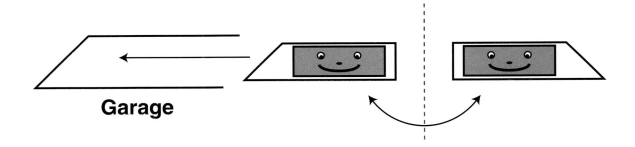

Garage

Professor Peabody Visits Flatville

Symmetry Game

This is a game for two players. You need pattern blocks and two sheets like this one to play.

Make a design with six pattern blocks on one side of the line on your sheet. This line will be the line of symmetry for a shape when you are done. Place blocks edge-to-edge. The edge of at least one block must touch the line.

Then, switch seats with your partner. Each player must place six blocks on the other side creating a shape with two matching halves.

Slide Design

Make a pattern block quilt design. Use slides to complete the quilt block. Work from Section 1 to 2 to 3 to 4. Trace around the pattern block shapes.

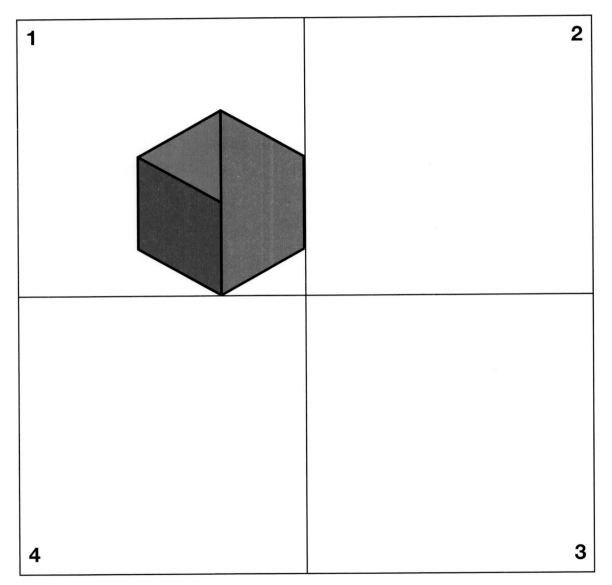

Checked by _____

Flip Design

Make a pattern block quilt design. Use flips to complete the quilt block. Work from Section 1 to 2 to 3 to 4. Trace around the pattern block shapes.

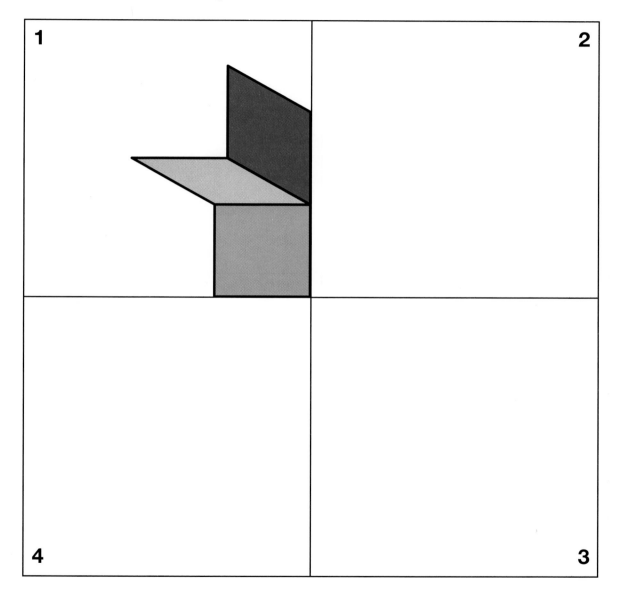

Checked by _____

My Quilt Block Design

I used _____ to complete the design.
(slides or flips)

1	**2**
4	**3**

Checked by _____

Name _____   Date _____

Turn Design

Make a pattern block quilt design. Use turns to complete the quilt block. Work from Section 1 to 2 to 3 to 4. Trace around the pattern block shapes.

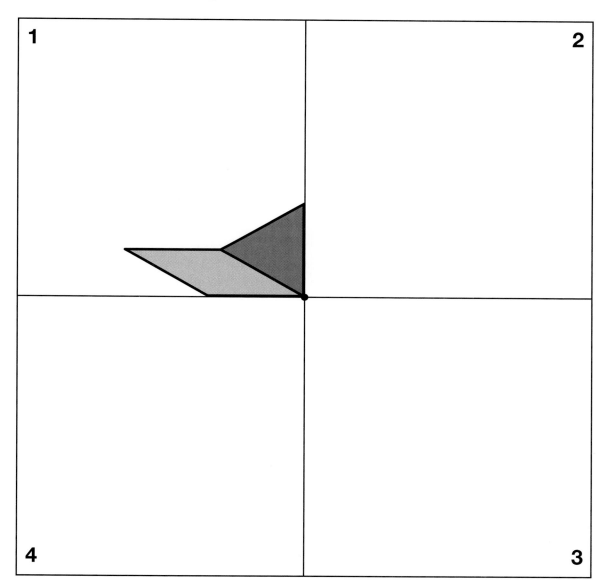

Checked by _____

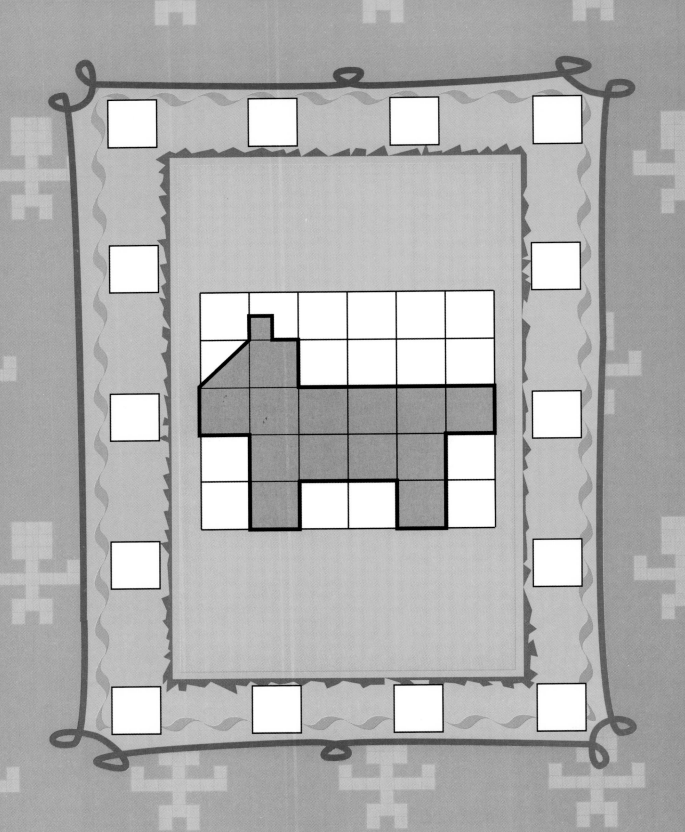

UNIT 16

Counting Area Practice

Count the area of the shapes. Label each shape with its area.

Introducing Area Measurement

Name _____ Date _____

Counting Area

Count the area of this shape.

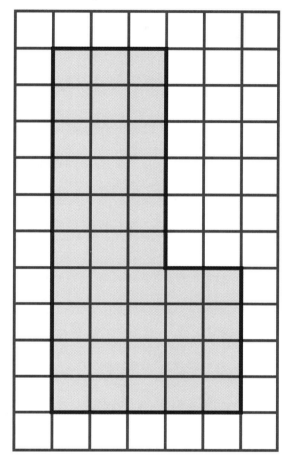

Area = _____ square centimeters

Square Centimeter Fractions

Write the area of each shape underneath it.

1.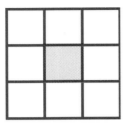

Area = _____

2.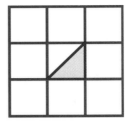

Area = _____

3.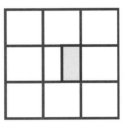

Area = _____

4.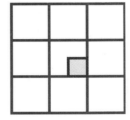

Area = _____

Shapes Grid

Find the area covered by each of the shapes shown below.

1.

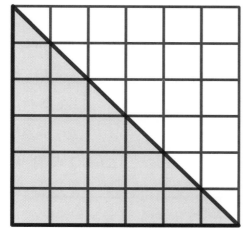

A = _____ sq cm

2.

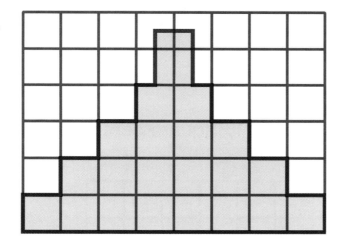

A = _____ sq cm

3.

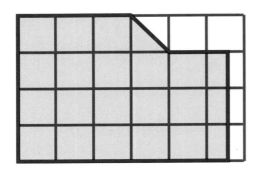

A = _____ sq cm

4.

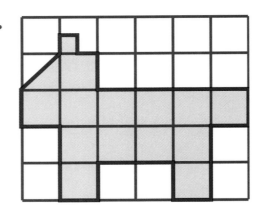

A = _____ sq cm

5.

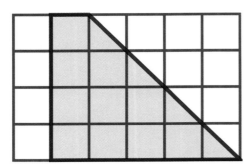

A = _____ sq cm

6.

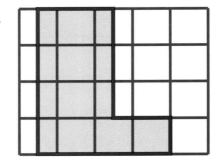

A = _____ sq cm

7. Draw a shape with an area of $11\frac{1}{2}$ square centimeters on the grid.

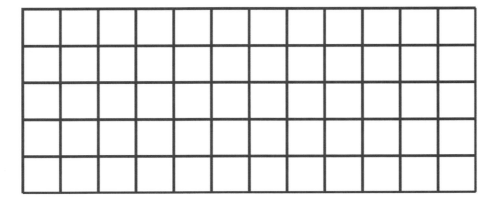

Counting Out Areas

Shapes Grid at Home

Homework

Find the area covered by each of the shapes shown below.

1.

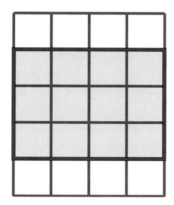

A = _____ sq cm

2.

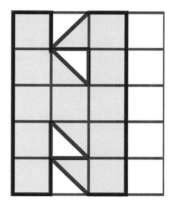

A = _____ sq cm

3.

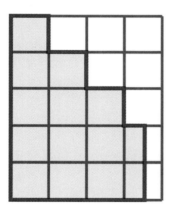

A = _____ sq cm

4.

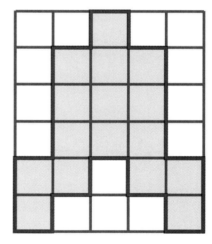

A = _____ sq cm

5.

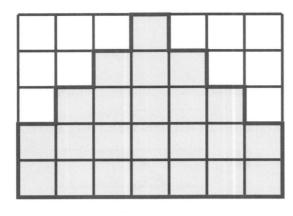

A = _____ sq cm

6.

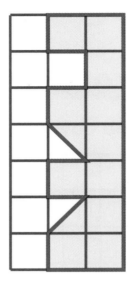

A = _____ sq cm

7.

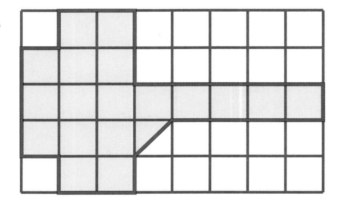

A = _____ sq cm

8. Draw a shape with an area of $9\frac{1}{4}$ sq centimeters.

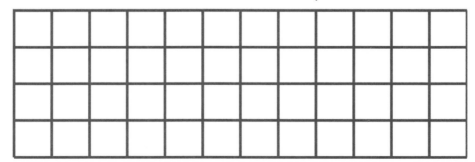

A = _____ sq cm

Counting Out Areas

Length, Width, and Area Rectangles

Find the length, width, and area of each of the shapes.

1.

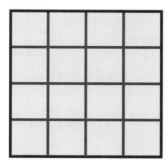

Length = _____ cm

Width = _____ cm

Area   = _____ sq cm

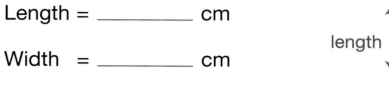

2.

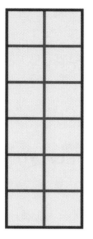

Length = _____ cm

Width = _____ cm

Area   = _____ sq cm

3.

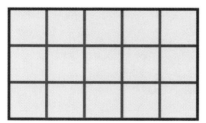

Length = _____ cm

Width = _____ cm

Area   = _____ sq cm

4. Which rectangle has the most area? _____

5. Does it have the largest length or width? _____

6.

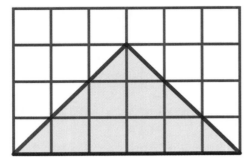

Length = _____ cm

Width = _____ cm

Area   = _____ sq cm

7.

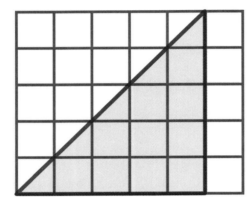

Length = _____ cm

Width = _____ cm

Area   = _____ sq cm

Length, Width, and Area

Length, Width, and Area Designs

Find the length, width, and area of each shape.

1.

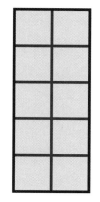

width

length

Length = _____ cm

Width = _____ cm

Area   = _____ sq cm

2.

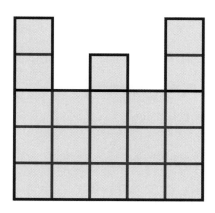

Length = _____ cm

Width = _____ cm

Area   = _____ sq cm

3.

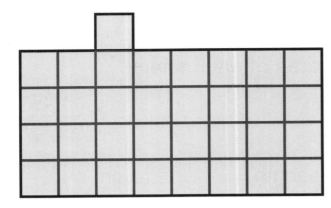

Length = _____ cm

Width = _____ cm

Area   = _____ sq cm

4.

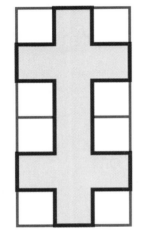

Area   = _____ sq cm

5.

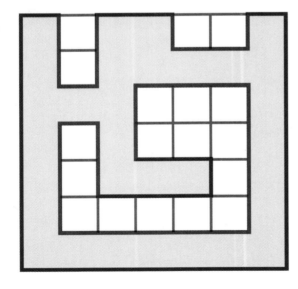

Area   = _____ sq cm

Area Riddles

For each riddle draw a shape and find its area.

1. My number of ▢ = 7

    My number of ◿ = 3

    My number of ▫ = 2

    What is my area? _____

2. My number of ▢ = 9

    My number of ◿ = 3

    My number of ▫ = 3

    What is my area? _____

3. My number of ▢ = 6

    My number of ◿ = 5

    My number of ▫ = 1

    What is my area? _____

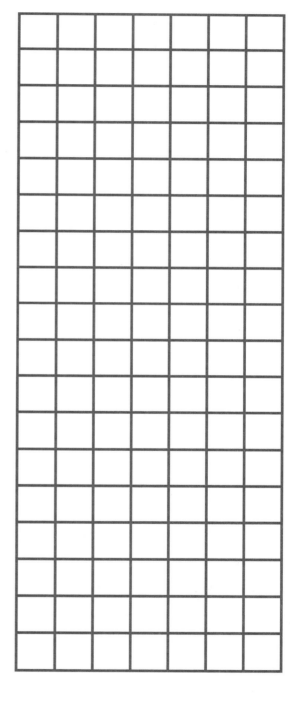

Area Questions

How are Shapes A and B alike and different?

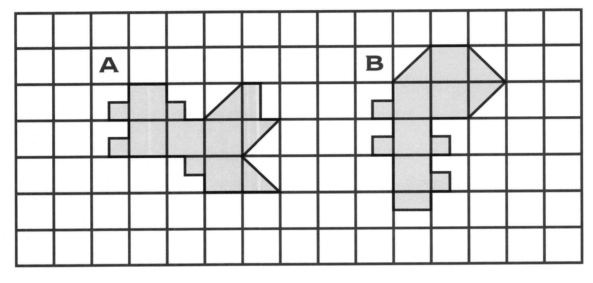

_____

_____

_____

_____   _____

_____

What is the area of Shape A? _____

What is the area of Shape B? _____

Area Hunt

Make rectangles on your geoboard that match the areas shown. You may not be able to make rectangles for some of the areas. Which areas can you get in more than one way? If you find more than one way, use the geoboard on the following page for the extra shapes.

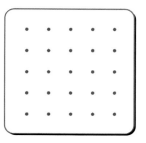

Area = 1 square unit

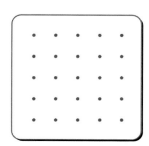

Area = 2 square units

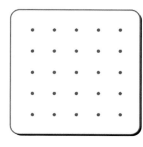

Area = 3 square units

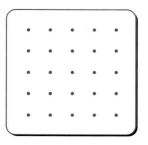

Area = 4 square units

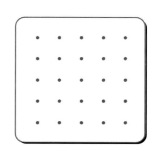

Area = 5 square units

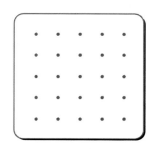

Area = 6 square units

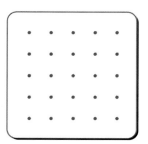

Area = 7 square units

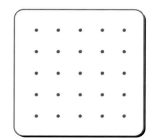

Area = 8 square units

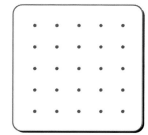

Area = 9 square units

For extra shapes:

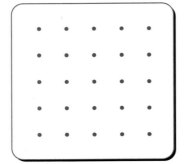

Area = _____

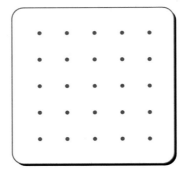

Area = _____

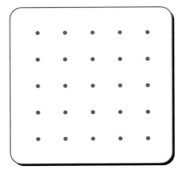

Area = _____

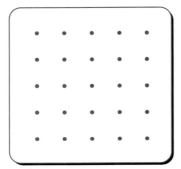

Area = _____

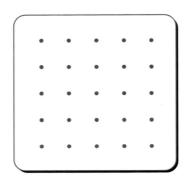

Area = _____

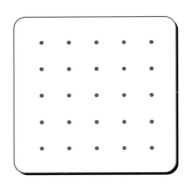

Area = _____

Area and the Geoboard

Geoboard Areas

Make these shapes on the geoboard. Find the area of each shape. Don't forget to write down the units.

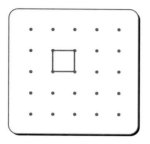

Area = _____

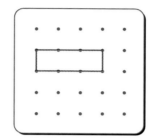

Area = _____

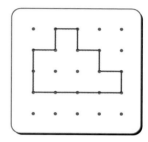

Area = _____

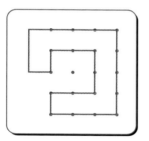

Area = _____

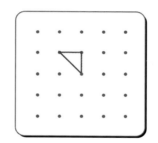

Area = _____

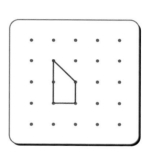

Area = _____

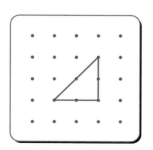

Area = _____

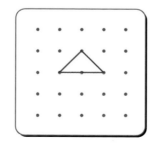

Area = _____

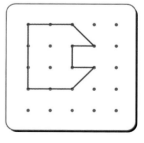

Area = _____

More Geoboard Puzzles

See how many of these geoboard puzzles you can solve on the geoboard. Then, draw the shape. If you can, use the second geoboard for a different answer.

1. A square with an area of 9 square units

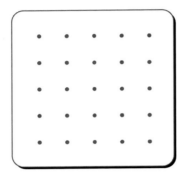 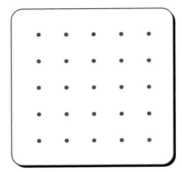

2. A rectangle with an area of 12 square units

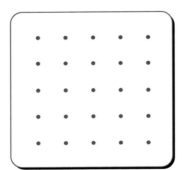 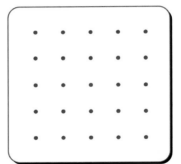

3. A rectangle with an area of 8 square units

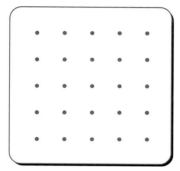
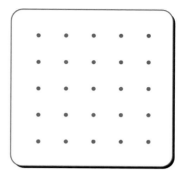

4. A rectangle with an area of 6 square units

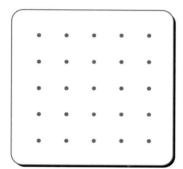
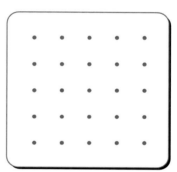

5. A rectangle with an area of 16 square units

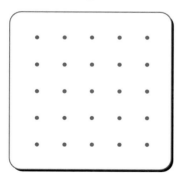
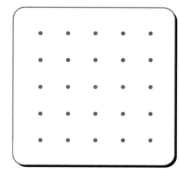

UNIT 17

3-D Shape Hunt

Look for these three-dimensional shapes in the classroom:

sphere   cube   cylinder   rectangular prism

cone   rectangular pyramid   triangular pyramid   triangular prism

Record the object and its shape in the data table.

3-D Shape Hunt Data Table

Object	3-D Shape

Exploring 3-D Shapes

Alike and Different

Draw your two shapes below and label them.

1. How are your two shapes alike?

   _____

   _____

   _____

2. How are your two shapes different?

   _____

   _____

   _____

Name _____ Date _____

Describing Geometric Solids

1. What is your 3-D shape? _____

2. Write as many ways as you can think of to describe your shape.

_____

_____

_____

_____

_____

_____

_____

_____

_____

_____

_____

Edges, Vertices, and Faces

Look at each skeleton of a solid that you made. How many edges, vertices, and faces does each 3-D shape have? Record the number on the data table.

Skeletons of Solids Data Table

Type of Solid	Number of Edges	Number of Vertices	Number of Faces
cube			
triangular prism			
rectangular pyramid			
triangular pyramid			
rectangular prism			

Faces, Edges, and Vertices

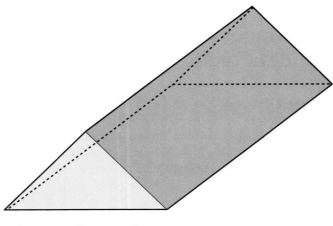

triangular prism

1. How many faces does it have?

_____

2. How many edges does it have?

_____

3. How many vertices does it have?

_____

4. What makes it a triangular prism?

_____

_____

_____

_____

Skeletons of Solids

City of the Future Data Table

How many of each 3-D shape did you use in your city of the future? Record the number in the data table.

City of the Future Data Table

Type of 3-D Shape	Number
cube	
cone	
cylinder	
hemisphere	
rectangular prism	
rectangular pyramid	
sphere	
triangular prism	
triangular pyramid	

UNIT 18

Mr. O's Data Table

Look at Mr. O's Map. Tell where each shape is.

Shape	Distance (in ___cm___)	Direction
triangle ▼	7	R
square ◆		
rhombus ◆		
hexagon ⬡		

Meet Mr. O and Mr. O's Map

Where Are They?

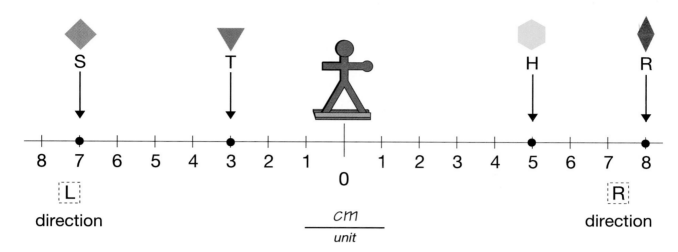

direction   L   8 7 6 5 4 3 2 1 0 1 2 3 4 5 6 7 8   R   direction

$$\frac{cm}{unit}$$

1. How far and in what direction is the triangle from Mr. O?

    _____   _____
    Distance   Direction

2. Where is the rhombus? _____   _____
                          Distance   Direction

3. What is the distance between the rhombus and the

   hexagon? _____

4. Distance between triangle and square? _____

5. Distance between triangle and hexagon? _____

Ada's Kitchen

- When visiting Ada's house Daryl saw that there were six chairs around her kitchen table.

- Daryl found the dog dish when he accidentally stepped into it. The dog dish was in front of the stove.

- The stove and refrigerator were next to each other, along the same wall as the sink.

- The windowsill took up about half of the right wall.

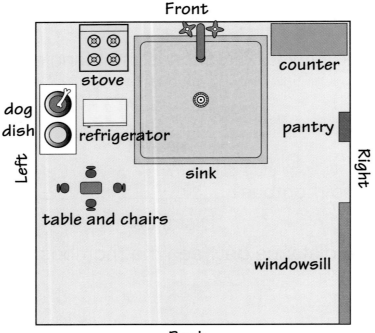

Front

Back

Left

Right

stove

dog dish

refrigerator

counter

pantry

sink

table and chairs

windowsill

Discuss

1. Does Daryl's map match what he saw in the kitchen? Explain.

2. Compare the sizes of the objects. Does the map seem right? What would you change about Daryl's map?

Classroom Map

Work with your group to discuss the size and location of various objects in your classroom. Then, work alone to make a list of the objects you will include in your map. When drawing your map:

- Put objects in the **right place** compared to one another.
- Try to make the objects the **right size**.
- Label the objects that you draw.
- When you are finished, compare your map with the maps your group members created.

List the objects you plan to include on your classroom map.

1. _____ Mr. O _____

2. _Classroom door_

3. _____

4. _____

5. _____

6. _____

7. _____

8. _____

Name _____ Date _____

Answer the following questions:

1. Is the teacher's desk bigger or smaller than the other desks?

_____

2. Tell which objects are located in the…

A. Front of the room _____

B. Back of the room _____

C. Middle of the room _____

D. Right side of the room _____

E. Left side of the room _____

_____

_____

_____

_____

My Classroom Map

Front

Left

Right

Back

Meter Square

Below is a picture of a square on the floor. In the square are two paste jars, a math book, one rubber band, one calculator, one Mr. O, two pencils, and two cups.

Work in groups. Make a square on the floor as shown in the picture. Then, place the other objects on the floor as they appear in the picture.

Front

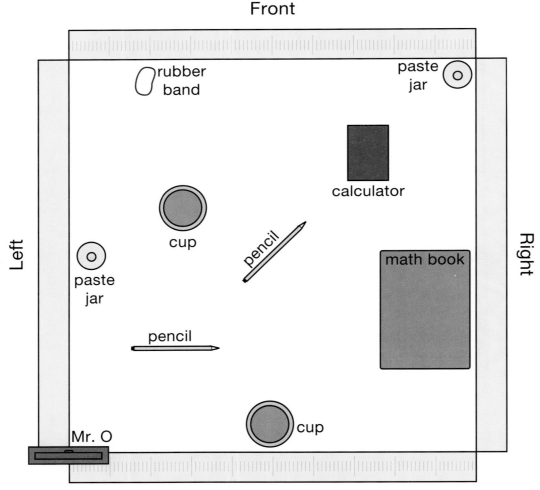

Left

Right

rubber band

paste jar

calculator

cup

pencil

paste jar

pencil

math book

Mr. O

cup

Back

How to Make Rain Forest Trails

This is how you make your rain forest animals.

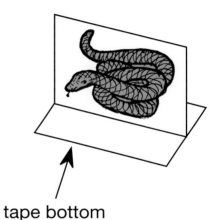

Snake

↑ fold up   ↑ fold down   ↑ fold up

Make sure there is at least one animal in every direction from Mr. O.

Tape the parrot and the snake to Mr. O's right.

Tape the turtle to Mr. O's left.

Place the animals crosswise on the axes trails.

tape bottom

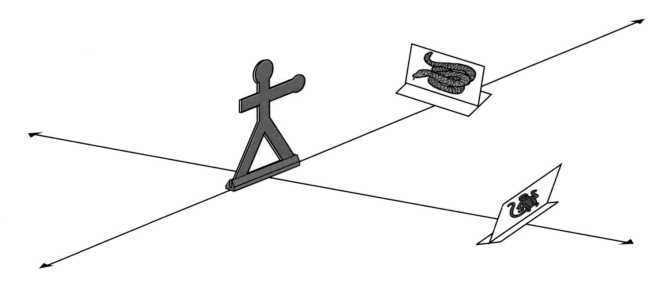

Rain Forest Trails Data Table

Record the distance and direction of your rain forest animals in the data table.

Rain Forest Trails Data Table
Mr. O Setup # _____

Animal	Distance (in _____) *unit*	Direction
armadillo		
spider monkey		
howler monkey		
parrot		R
turtle		L
snake		R

Mr. O Left/Right or Front/Back

Draw

Draw a picture of your lab setup. Be sure to label the axes left, right, front, and back.

Name _____   Date _____

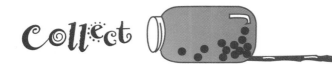 Collect

Work with your group to fill in the data table.

Mr. O Left/Right or Front/Back Data Table
Mr. O Setup # _____
Mapping Group

Animal	Distance (in _____)	Direction
armadillo		
spider monkey		
howler monkey		
parrot		
turtle		
snake		

Map

Look at the data table. Decide as a group how to number the lines on the map. Then, plot the animals on the map.

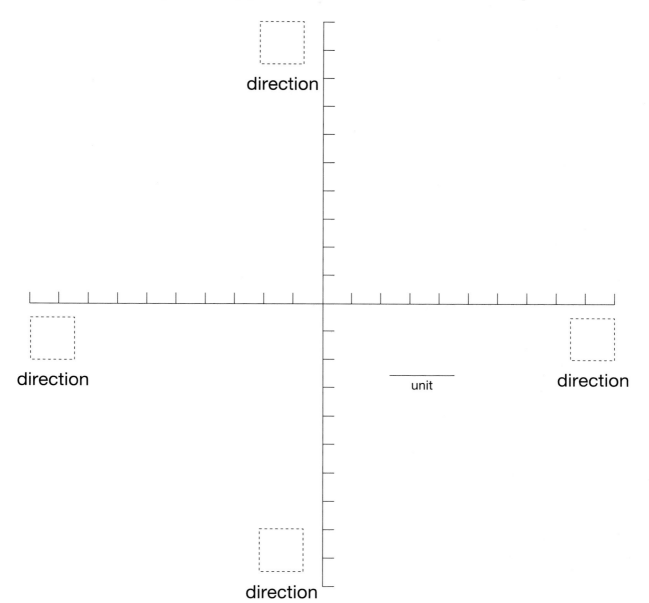

1. **A.** Use your map or data table to predict how far the parrot is from the turtle.

_____

B. How did you find the answer? _____

C. Now measure the distance from the parrot to the turtle. Is your answer the same as your prediction?

_____

2. **A.** What animal is the farthest from the front of Mr. O?

_____

B. How far from his front is it? _____

3. **A.** What animal is the farthest from the back of Mr. O?

_____

B. How far from his back is it? _____

4. What is the distance between these two animals?

_____

Name _____   Date _____

Mr. O Map and Data Tables

Part 1

Here is Mr. O in a field. There is a front/back line and a right/left line. Fill in the data table.

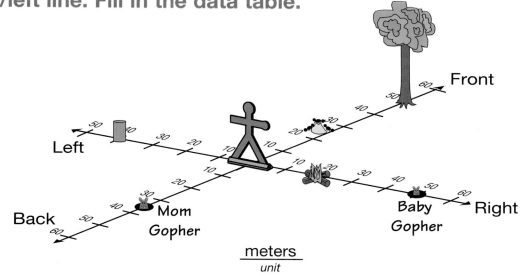

$$\dfrac{\text{meters}}{\text{unit}}$$

Mr. O in the Field Data Table

Object	Distance (in _____) *unit*	Direction
can		
campfire		
anthill		
oak tree		
baby gopher		

1. Baby gopher is lost. Tell Mom gopher how to get to him.

_____

_____

2. How far is the tree from the anthill? _____

3. How far is it from the campfire to the can? _____

4. How could you travel from the campfire to the anthill?

_____

_____

Part 2

Ivana has a Mr. O on her desk. She uses a ruler to measure distances. Here is her data table.

Ivana's Data Table

Object	Distance (in ___cm___) unit	Direction
A. Marble	8 cm	R
B. Penny	8 cm	L
C. Washer	5 cm	R

Name _____ Date _____

Draw the marble, penny, and washer on the map below.

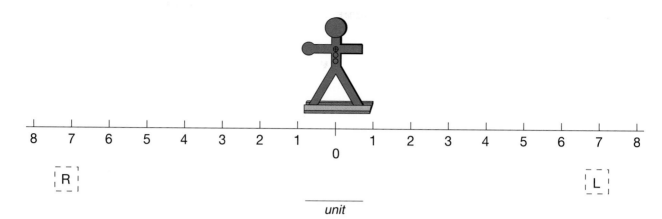

8 7 6 5 4 3 2 1 | 1 2 3 4 5 6 7 8
0

R   L

_____
unit

1. How far is the marble from the washer? _____

2. How far is the penny from the marble? _____

3. How far is the penny from the washer? _____

4. Which object is closest to Mr. O? _____

5. Which object is farthest from Mr. O? _____

6. Which object is the farthest to the right? _____

7. Which object is the farthest to the left? _____

UNIT 19

Counting Kids

Draw

Draw a picture of the survey. Show what information you are looking for and how you might find it.

I predict that the most likely number of kids is _____.

Counting Kids Data Table

Number of _____	Number of _____		
	Tallies		Total
1			
2			
3			
4			
5			
6			
7			
8			
9			
10			
11			
	Total Number of Families		

 Graph

On a separate piece of graph paper, make a bar graph of your data from the table. Label the axes and number the lines. Then, fill in the bars.

 Explore

Work with a partner to answer Questions 1–7.

1. What is the total number of families? _____

2. What is half of the total number of families? _____

3. How many families have more than 3 kids? _____

4. **A.** How many families have three or more kids?

   _____

   B. Is this more or fewer than half of all the families?

   _____

5. **A.** How many families have fewer than three kids?

   _____

   B. Is this more or fewer than half of all the families?

   _____

6. What is the range of the number of kids?

_____ to _____

(This is the smallest to the largest number.)

7. What number of kids occurs most often? _____

(This is the most likely number of kids in a family.)

8. Compare your family with the other families in your class.

A. How many kids are in your family? _____

B. How many families have more kids than yours?

_____

C. How many other families have the same number of kids as yours?

_____

D. How many families have fewer kids than yours?

_____

9. Does your family have more, fewer, or the same number of kids than the most likely number of kids found in the survey?

_____

Comparing Graphs

Kathy and Andy attend different schools. Information about their classes is shown in the graphs below.

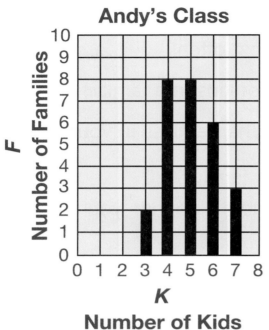

Andy's Class

F — Number of Families
K — Number of Kids

Kathy's Class

F — Number of Families
K — Number of Kids

1. What is the most likely number of kids in a family in Andy's class?

_____

2. A. Which class has the bigger range of kids in a family?

_____

B. What is the range of kids for that class?

_____

3. A. Which class has more families? _____

    B. How many more families?

_____

    C. Explain how you found your answer. _____

_____

_____

4. Find a way that either class's graph looks like your class's graph. Tell how they are alike.

_____

_____

_____

_____

Doubling Machine and Input-Output Data Table

Complete the table for the Doubling Machine.

Input-Output Data Table

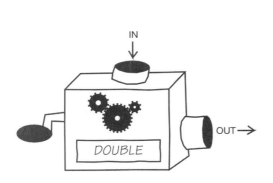

Input	Output
12	
5	
24	
17	
43	
31	

You have a machine that you can use as a Doubling Machine. What is it?

Use this machine to double the numbers in the table. Does your machine give the same answers that you did?

Target Numbers–Finding Half

Work with a partner, and use Rosa and Scottie's guess-and-check method to find half of the target number.

Target Number 136

Input	Output	Next Guess – *Higher or Lower*

Target Number 278

Input	Output	Next Guess – *Higher or Lower*

Input-Output

Complete these tables for the two Function Machines. The rule is given for the first table. Find the rule for the second table.

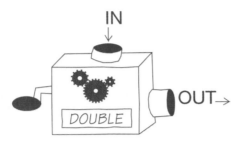

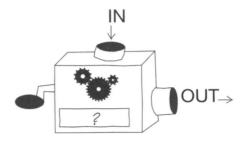

Rule:

Double

Input	Output
3	
8	
	18
23	
	70
125	

Rule:

Input	Output
5	14
7	16
8	17
	18
	20
21	

Name _____ Date _____

L-Gator

The L-gator is only one square when it is one year old.

It has no teeth at first, but by the second year it grows two teeth.

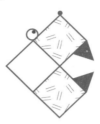

1. How many squares does an L-Gator have when it is two

years old? _____

By the third year, the L-gator looks a little dangerous.

2. How many teeth does a three-year-old L-Gator have?

_____

3. How many squares does a three-year-old L-Gator have?

_____

4. How many teeth does an L-Gator grow each year?

_____

5. Without drawing a five-year-old L-Gator, could you tell how many teeth and squares it would have? _____

6. How can you find out? _____

_____

7. How old is this L-Gator? _____

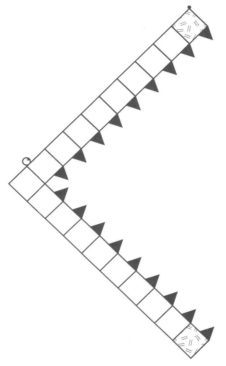

8. How old would an L-gator be if it had 21 squares? _____

9. How old would an L-gator be if it had 51 squares? _____

10. How could you find out how many teeth and squares a 100-year-old L-Gator would have? _____

_____

Three-Winged Blue Bird

The Three-Winged Blue Bird has four squares when it is one year old.

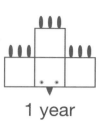

1 year   2 years

1. How many squares does it have when it is two years old?

_____

2. How many squares does a Three-Winged Blue Bird grow

each year? _____

3. Draw a five-year-old Three-Winged Blue Bird.

4. How many squares does a ten-year-old Three-Winged Blue

Bird have? _____ Show your work.

5. How old is a Three-Winged Blue Bird with 40 squares?

_____ Show your work.

Double Worm

This is how a One-Eyed Double Worm looks when it is born.

The next year, the One-Eyed Double Worm is twice as large.

The year after that, it doubles in length again.

It keeps on growing, getting twice as large every year.

1. Do you think a One-Eyed Double Worm as old as you would

   be very big? _____ Explain. _____

   _____

   _____

2. How long would a ten-year-old One-Eyed Double Worm be?

   _____ Show your work.

3. Would you like to meet a One-Eyed Double Worm that is 50

years old? _____ Explain. _____

_____

_____

There are many kinds of Double Worms on Gzorp. All the different kinds of Double Worms grow twice as long every year. Double Worms always grow in a straight line. Here is a one-year-old Three-Eyed Double Worm.

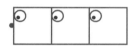

4. Draw a picture of the Three-Eyed Double Worm when it is two years old.

5. How many squares will it have when it is five years old?

_____ Show your work.

6. How old is a Three-Eyed Double Worm with 96 squares?

_____ Show your work.

7. How many squares will it have when it is seven years old?

_____ Show your work.

Berry Drink

For one serving:

$\frac{1}{4}$ cup fresh strawberries

$\frac{1}{3}$ cup white grape juice

$\frac{1}{4}$ cup raspberry sherbet

$\frac{1}{4}$ tablespoon lemon juice

3 ice cubes (optional)

Mix all ingredients in a blender.

UNIT 20

How Many Inches?

Measure the following distances to the nearest quarter inch. First, each partner makes a measurement. If your measurements differ, measure again and decide on a correct measurement.

Object	Kind of Measurement	Partner 1's Measurement (in inches)	Partner 2's Measurement (in inches)	Agreed Measurement (in inches)
one person's thumb	length			
scissors	length			
this paper	length			
	width			
one person's foot	length			
math book	perimeter			
door	width			

Useful Fractions

Berry Drink

Use the one-serving recipe to make two- and three-serving recipes.

Berry Drink

For one serving:

$\frac{1}{4}$ cup fresh strawberries

$\frac{1}{3}$ cup white grape juice

$\frac{1}{4}$ cup raspberry sherbet

$\frac{1}{4}$ tablespoon lemon juice

3 ice cubes (optional)

Mix all ingredients in a blender.

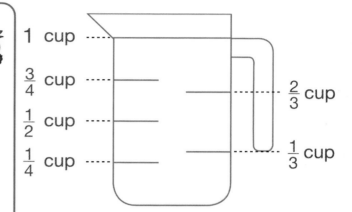

1 cup

$\frac{3}{4}$ cup

$\frac{1}{2}$ cup

$\frac{1}{4}$ cup

$\frac{2}{3}$ cup

$\frac{1}{3}$ cup

Berry Drink

For two servings:

_____ fresh strawberries

_____ white grape juice

_____ raspberry sherbet

_____ lemon juice

_____ ice cubes

Berry Drink

For three servings:

_____ fresh strawberries

_____ white grape juice

_____ raspberry sherbet

_____ lemon juice

_____ ice cubes

Nailing It Down

1. Mr. Robinson, the carpenter, needs help sorting his nails. This is a life-size picture of the nails. How long is each nail in inches? (Measure to the nearest quarter inch.)

A. _____

B. _____

C. _____

D. _____

2. Grandpa and Willie are repairing a fence. They need a board that is 36 inches long. They have only a 1-foot ruler. How many times does Grandpa need to use the ruler? Explain how you found your answer.

_____

_____

_____

_____

_____

Fraction Trains

Use connecting cubes to answer each question. Draw pictures of the connecting cubes for each problem.

1. Make a train with 3 green and 1 red connecting cubes.

    A. What fraction of the train is green? _____

    B. What fraction of the train is red? _____

2. Make a train with 3 blue and 3 white connecting cubes.

    A. What fraction of the train is blue? _____

    B. What fraction of the train is white? _____

    C. What other fraction shows what part is white? _____

3. Make a train of 5 connecting cubes that is $\frac{3}{5}$ blue and the rest is red.

    A. How many connecting cubes are blue? _____

    B. How many connecting cubes are white? _____

    C. What fraction of the train is red? _____

4. Make a train with 3 green, 3 blue, 3 white, and 3 red connecting cubes.

    A. What fraction does each color show? _____

    B. What fraction is green and blue? _____

    C. Can you think of some other fractions that describe parts of this train? Make a list of all the fractions you can find. Tell why each fraction fits some part of this train.

    _____

    _____

Name _____ Date _____

Fraction Circles

There are 4 circles below. Color the circles to show $\frac{3}{4}$.

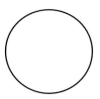 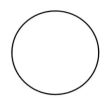 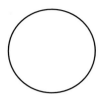

What did you do to show $\frac{3}{4}$? _____

_____

Explain how you know your picture is correct.

_____

_____

_____

_____

_____

_____

Geoboard Halves

Work with a partner. Make this rectangle on your geoboard.

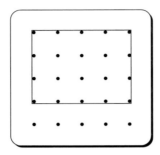

How many ways can you find to divide this rectangle into halves? Record each way you find below.

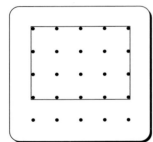 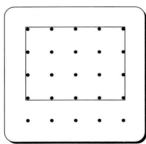 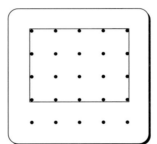 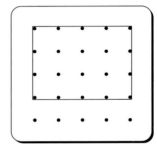

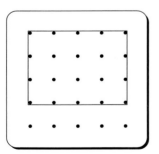 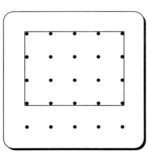 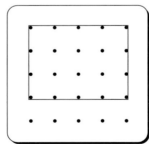 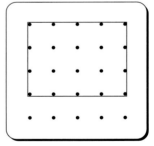

Geoboard Fractions

Geoboard Thirds

Cross out the geoboards below that do not show this shape divided into thirds.

Choose one of the geoboards you crossed out. Explain why it does not show thirds.

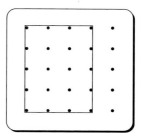

_____

_____

_____

_____

1. 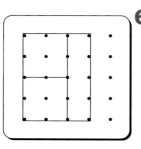   **2.** 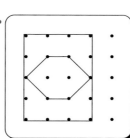   **3.** 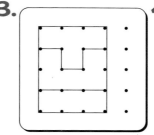   **4.**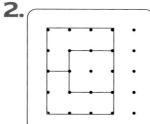

5. 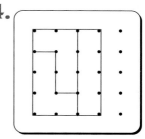   **6.** 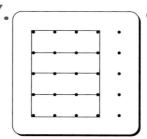   **7.** 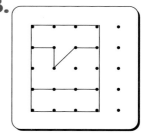   **8.**